I0421922

TWELVE POINTS OF VIEW

It comprises twelve interdisciplinary strategic briefs spanning Economics, Neuropsychology, International Law, Public Policy, and Cultural Diplomacy.

With Additional Readings for Further Insight and Practice.

Author: Mosi Dorbayani, MBA, LLM, MSc, PhD

Chartered Psychologist (BPS);
Chartered Manager (CIM);
Chartered Professional in Human Resources (CPHR)

Member of:
Canadian Psychological Association (CPA).
International Bar Association (IBA – Law); and,
The Academic Council on The United Nations System (ACUNS).

Orenda Publications and WAALM Publications.

Library & Archive Canada ISBN: 978-1-0688715-3-5

Each briefing is also available in Kindle Edition by the same publishers.

Each Briefing Stands Alone, and Can Be Read Independently.

This book is dedicated to you.

"The biggest challenge for human being is human being. How to understand and being understood, how to love and being loved."

Mosi Dorbayani

Contents:

Foreword:

Interdisciplinary work is not an academic luxury; it is an intellectual necessity. In bringing together twelve strategic briefs that traverse Economics, Neuropsychology, International Law, Public Policy, and Cultural Diplomacy, this volume models the kind of integrative thinking our complex world demands. Each brief is a focused inquiry, and together they form a lattice of perspectives that strengthens analysis, sharpens policy relevance, and accelerates practical impact.

For society, the value is immediate and tangible. Problems such as economic inequality, mental health in post-conflict settings, transnational regulatory gaps, and cultural misunderstanding do not respect disciplinary boundaries. When economists, neuropsychologists, legal scholars, and cultural diplomats speak to one another, solutions become more humane, more implementable, and more durable. Policymakers and practitioners gain tools that are evidence informed, context sensitive, and ethically grounded.

For science, interdisciplinarity expands the horizon of inquiry. It invites new hypotheses, novel methods, and

1

richer datasets. Neuropsychological insights can refine economic models of decision making. Legal frameworks can be tested against behavioral evidence. Cultural diplomacy can be evaluated with quantitative and qualitative rigor. This cross-fertilization accelerates discovery and reduces the blind spots that arise when fields operate in isolation.

For scholarly endeavor, the collection cultivates a practice-based approach that encourages deeper engagement across fields. It rewards scholars who translate their work for other audiences and who listen as much as they argue. It creates pedagogical opportunities for training researchers who are fluent in multiple vocabularies and comfortable at the interfaces where real-world problems live. It also models scholarly humility by showing how modest, well-argued briefs can influence debate more effectively than sprawling, insular treatises. Readers will find here not only analyses but pathways: pathways to collaboration, to policy change, and to research that matters. May this collection inspire further conversations across disciplines and sustained commitments to scholarship that serves the public good.

Briefing 1.

THE MOST HANGING QUESTION IN PUBLIC FINANCE AND POLITICAL ECONOMY

In Brief:

The most enduring and unresolved tension at the heart of modern governance can be distilled into a single, deceptively simple question: ***How can democratic governments design and sustain fiscal systems that balance long-term public investment with short-term political incentives?*** As a certified Public Financial Manager, Public Policy Scholar, and an Economist, I believe this question persists because it sits precisely at the intersection of public finance and political economy, where the logic of economic stewardship collides with the realities of democratic politics.

Public finance, at its core, demands intertemporal discipline. Governments must raise revenue, allocate spending, and manage debt in ways that ensure stability not only today but decades into the future. Infrastructure, education, climate resilience, and technological innovation all require sustained investment whose benefits unfold slowly. Yet democratic politics operates on compressed timelines. Electoral cycles, partisan competition, and interest-group pressures create incentives for policymakers

4

to prioritize immediate gains over long-term welfare. *This structural misalignment—between what is economically optimal and what is politically feasible—forms the backbone of the "hanging question" that continues to shape fiscal debates worldwide.*

The Challenge: Is It Technical or Philosophical?

The challenge is compounded by demographic and economic pressures. Aging populations increase demand for pensions and healthcare while shrinking the tax base. Rising inequality fuels political polarization around taxation and redistribution. Public debt, accumulated through decades of crisis response and political compromise, constrains fiscal space. These pressures intensify the need for long-term planning even as they make such planning more politically costly.

Political economy research shows that fiscal outcomes are rarely the product of economic logic alone. They emerge from institutional design, coalition dynamics, and ideological contestation. Countries facing similar shocks often adopt radically different fiscal strategies because their

5

political structures channel incentives differently. Some systems encourage consensus-building and long-term planning; others reward short-term distributive politics. This diversity makes it difficult to identify a universal model of fiscal governance, reinforcing the unresolved nature of the central question.

Ultimately, the issue is not merely technical but philosophical. *It asks whether societies can align collective long-term welfare with the short-term incentives of political actors.* It challenges democracies to reconcile the needs of future generations with the demands of present voters. And it forces policymakers to confront the uncomfortable truth that fiscal sustainability is as much a political achievement as an economic one.

Every major debate in public finance—debt sustainability, tax reform, welfare design, climate investment, and state capacity—circles back to this same unresolved tension. Until democratic institutions find ways to reward long-term stewardship, the question will remain hanging, shaping the trajectory of public policy across generations.

Institutional Design Levers:

A critical yet often underemphasized dimension of fiscal governance lies in the architecture of institutions that shape political incentives. Well-designed fiscal frameworks can create guardrails that discipline short-term political behaviour without undermining democratic legitimacy. Multi-year budgeting systems, for example, extend the planning horizon beyond electoral cycles, forcing governments to internalize the long-term consequences of today's decisions. Independent revenue-forecasting bodies reduce optimism bias and prevent politically motivated manipulation of fiscal baselines. Fiscal rules—particularly those with transparent escape clauses—can anchor expectations while preserving flexibility during crises. These institutional levers do not eliminate political incentives, but they recalibrate them, making long-term stewardship more feasible within democratic constraints.

Public Trust and Legitimacy:

No fiscal system, however technically sound, can endure without public trust. Legitimacy shapes the political space in which long-term decisions are made, influencing everything from tax compliance to support for structural reforms. When citizens believe that fiscal burdens are distributed fairly and that public resources are managed responsibly, they are more willing to accept policies whose benefits accrue gradually. Conversely, low trust amplifies resistance to necessary but politically costly measures, such as pension reform or climate investment. Transparent communication, participatory budgeting, and clear reporting on long-term outcomes can strengthen the social contract, reducing the political cost of long-horizon policymaking. In this sense, fiscal sustainability is inseparable from democratic legitimacy.

Behavioural Political Economy:

The tension between long-term public investment and short-term political incentives is not only structural—it is psychological. Voters, like policymakers, exhibit present bias, overweighting immediate costs and undervaluing distant benefits. Politicians, facing electoral pressures, respond rationally to these behavioural tendencies, often prioritizing policies that deliver quick, visible gains. Loss aversion further complicates reform efforts, as citizens tend to resist changes that impose short-term sacrifices even when long-term welfare improves. Recognizing these behavioural dynamics allows policymakers to design reforms that are politically viable—for example, by sequencing benefits earlier, framing policies in terms of avoided losses, or using default mechanisms that nudge long-term compliance. Behavioural political economy thus provides a crucial lens for understanding why long-term fiscal governance remains elusive.

State Capacity and Implementation Risk:

Even the most elegant fiscal frameworks falter without strong state capacity. Effective long-term planning requires reliable data systems, competent public administration, and coordination across multiple levels of government. Weak administrative capacity can distort projections, delay implementation, and erode public confidence. Fragmented governance—particularly in federal systems—creates misaligned incentives and complicates the execution of long-term investment strategies. Digital infrastructure, workforce capability, and institutional memory all shape a government's ability to sustain policies across political cycles. For public policy architects, strengthening state capacity is not a peripheral concern but a foundational requirement for any credible long-term fiscal strategy.

Comparative Global Insights:

A comparative perspective reveals that while the tension between long-term investment and short-term politics is universal, institutional responses vary widely. Consensus-oriented political cultures, such as those in Nordic countries, tend to support stable, long-horizon fiscal planning through broad coalitions and social compacts. East Asian developmental states have historically relied on technocratic insulation to prioritize long-term national objectives. Westminster systems, with their adversarial politics and rapid policy swings, often struggle to maintain continuity. Federal systems face coordination challenges that complicate national investment strategies. These contrasts illustrate that there is no single model of fiscal governance; instead, institutional design must reflect political culture, administrative capacity, and historical context.

Emerging Pressures and Future Constraints:

Looking ahead, emerging structural pressures will intensify the need for long-term fiscal governance while making it more politically challenging. Climate-related shocks will impose unpredictable fiscal burdens, requiring governments to invest in resilience even as voters prioritize immediate affordability. AI-driven labour market disruptions will reshape tax bases and social protection systems, demanding anticipatory policy design. Demographic realignment, including aging populations and migration flows, will alter the distribution of fiscal burdens across generations. The rise of intangible capital complicates traditional taxation models, challenging governments to modernize revenue systems. These pressures underscore that the unresolved tension at the heart of public finance is not static—it is evolving, and the cost of inaction will only grow.

Policy Recommendations: Making Consequences Visible

1. **Establish Independent Long-Term Fiscal Councils with Binding Mandates**

   Create nonpartisan institutions empowered to evaluate fiscal plans, enforce sustainability rules, and publish long-horizon projections. By shifting some decisions outside short-term political cycles, governments can anchor policy in long-term evidence while preserving democratic accountability.

2. **Introduce Intergenerational Impact Statements for Major Legislation**

   Require every significant fiscal bill to include a transparent assessment of its effects on future generations—covering debt, climate, infrastructure, and demographic implications. This reframes political debate, making long-term consequences visible and politically salient.

Beyond Policy:

Beyond the above policy recommendations, there are a number of elements that entities and firms engaged in Macro and Micro-economy perhaps need to address:

What Entities Engaged at Macro Level May Need to Address:

Those operating at a macro-economic scale—multinationals, major financial institutions, infrastructure actors, and system-shaping industries—must navigate forces that influence entire national or global economies.

1. Long-Horizon Investment Under Policy Uncertainty

Large firms must plan capital allocation, R&D, and infrastructure investment across decades, yet fiscal and regulatory environments shift with political cycles. They must develop strategies that remain resilient despite fluctuating tax regimes, public debt levels, and government spending priorities.

2. Exposure to Systemic Risks

Macro-scale firms are directly affected by demographic shifts, inflation cycles, sovereign debt conditions, and global shocks. They must build capacity to anticipate and adapt to structural risks—aging populations, climate transitions, geopolitical fragmentation—that governments may under-address due to short-term incentives.

3. Alignment with National Development and Public Investment Agendas

Major firms increasingly operate in partnership with states. They must understand how public investment, infrastructure planning, and fiscal constraints shape long-term opportunities. Their competitiveness depends on anticipating how governments balance immediate political pressures with long-term national priorities.

What Firms Engaged at Micro Level May Need to Address:

Micro-economic firms—small and medium enterprises, local service providers, and niche producers—operate closer to households and individual markets. Their concerns are more immediate and operational.

1. Cost Structures and Consumer Behavior

Micro-firms must respond quickly to changes in wages, input prices, and household purchasing power. Inflation, taxation, and local regulation directly affect their margins and pricing strategies.

2. Market Competition and Differentiation

They must navigate competitive pressures, innovate in product offerings, and maintain customer loyalty. Micro-firms feel the effects of policy shifts more acutely because they lack the buffers of large corporations.

3. Regulatory Compliance and Administrative Burden

Local firms must manage licensing, taxation, reporting, and labor rules that may change with political cycles.

Their survival often depends on how efficiently they adapt to shifting micro-level regulatory environments.

The Critical Executive-Level Decisions:

To illuminate and navigate the unresolved tension—How can democratic governments design and sustain fiscal systems that balance long-term public investment with short-term political incentives? —executives must make decisions that bridge firm strategy with political-economic reality.

1. **Commit to Long-Term Strategic Planning Anchored in Scenario Analysis**

Executives must adopt planning frameworks that incorporate multiple political and fiscal futures. This reduces vulnerability to electoral volatility and positions the firm to thrive regardless of short-term policy swings.

2. **Engage in Structured Public–Private Dialogue**

Executives should participate in transparent, institutionalized channels with governments, industry associations, and civil society. This helps align private investment horizons with public investment cycles, reducing the mismatch between long-term economic needs and short-term political incentives.

3. Prioritize Investments that Complement Public Goods

Executives must identify where their firm's long-term interests align with societal long-term welfare—such as workforce development, climate resilience, digital infrastructure, and innovation ecosystems. These investments strengthen both firm competitiveness and national capacity, helping resolve the tension between immediate political pressures and enduring economic needs.

Conclusion:

The enduring tension between long-term public investment and short-term political incentives remains the central hanging question in public finance and political economy. Firms operating at both macro and micro levels feel the consequences of this misalignment in different but interconnected ways—whether through systemic risks, shifting regulatory landscapes, or the volatility of consumer demand. Executives, in turn, must navigate these dynamics with clarity, foresight, and strategic discipline.

By committing to long-horizon planning, engaging constructively with public institutions, and investing in areas that strengthen societal resilience, leaders can help bridge the gap between immediate political pressures and the enduring economic needs of future generations. The path forward requires not only technical expertise but a shared commitment to aligning private strategy with the long-term public good, ensuring that economic systems remain stable, adaptive, and capable of supporting sustainable growth.

Briefing 2.

THE COADUNATE ECONOMIC MODEL:
A REFLECTION IN MY OWN VOICE

In Brief:

Introducing The Model in Academic Term:

Although some time has passed since its original development and early application, I welcome this opportunity to revisit the model and articulate its underlying concept and intended strategic direction with greater clarity.

The Coadunate Economic Model emerges from the recognition that modern economies cannot thrive through isolated sectors, fragmented policies, or siloed institutional thinking. "Coadunate," meaning joined together for a common purpose, captures the essence of an economic architecture in which public institutions, private enterprise, civil society, and global partners operate in coordinated synergy. In academic terms, the Coadunate Economic Model emerges from the recognition that contemporary economies cannot be understood—let alone advanced—through isolated sectors or fragmented institutional thinking.

In academic terms, it is a systemic framework that positions economic vitality as the outcome of purposeful alignment among public institutions, private enterprise, civil society, and global partners. The model challenges the traditional compartmentalization of economic theory by proposing that prosperity is not merely the sum of discrete activities, but the product of their coherence.

At its core, the Coadunate Economic Model is a *strategic concept and practice* that catalyzes Business Economics, Talent Management, Cross-cultural dynamics—including the arts and creative industries—and Philanthropy to influence socio-economic outcomes in an emerging multi-polar world. I have long emphasized that the cultural and creative sectors are not peripheral to economic development. They are already dynamic drivers of economic activity and employment, particularly across North America and Europe. Cultural activities foster social inclusion, nurture diversity, and contribute meaningfully to reducing both physical and mental poverty.

Creative entrepreneurs, artists, writers, performers, and the vibrant cultural industries that support them are, in my view, unique sources of innovation essential for future sustainability. Their potential must be more fully recognized, valued, and actively explored by cultural practitioners, policymakers, and government agencies alike. When we harness the full capacity of culture, we empower societies to build a more inclusive and fairer world—one in which innovation, creativity, sustainability, and shared growth are not abstract aspirations but lived realities.

Culture promotes active citizenship and intercultural dialogue; it strengthens social cohesion and brings communities closer together. It supports the integration of refugees and migrants, fosters belonging, and enhances collective well-being. Ultimately, culture and the creative industries possess the transformative power to improve lives, revitalize communities, generate employment, stimulate economic growth, and influence a wide range of other sectors. In this sense, culture is not merely an accessory to development—it is one of its most vital engines.

Within this broader academic framing, the Coadunate Economic Model contributes a distinctive proposition: that economic systems flourish when their institutional, cultural, and human components move in concert. It is an economy conceived not as a mechanical structure, but as a living organism—dynamic, interdependent, and strengthened through cohesion.

This integrative perspective positions the model as both a theoretical contribution and a practical guide for nations seeking sustainable, human-centered development in a rapidly evolving global landscape.

It advances a distinct proposition: *economic vitality is not merely the sum of its parts, but the product of their alignment.*

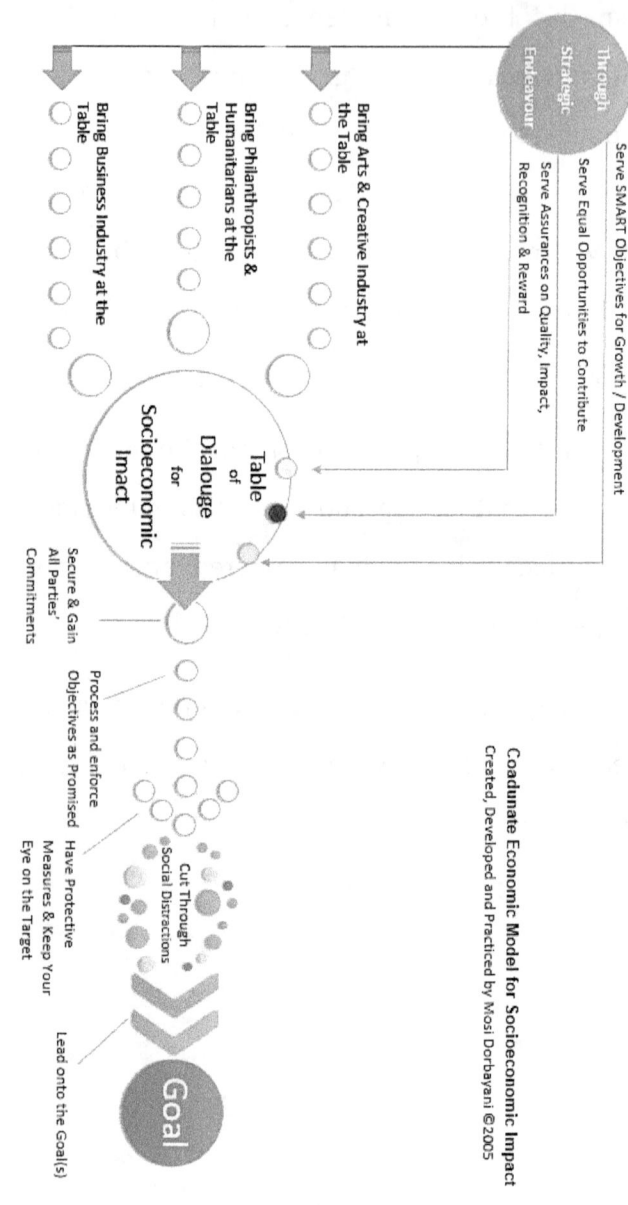

Coadunate Economic Model for Socioeconomic Impact
Created, Developed and Practiced by Mosi Dorbayani ©2005

Through Strategic Endeavour

Serve SMART Objectives for Growth / Development

Serve Equal Opportunities to Contribute

Serve Assurances on Quality, Impact, Recognition & Reward

Bring Arts & Creative Industry at the Table

Bring Philanthropists & Humanitarians at the Table

Bring Business Industry at the Table

Table of Dialouge for Socioeconomic Imact

Secure & Gain All Parties' Commitments

Process and enforce Objectives as Promised

Cut Through Social Distractions

Have Protective Measures & Keep Your Eye on the Target

Lead onto the Goal(s)

Goal

24

Connecting the Model with Industry Practice:

In industry, the Coadunate Economic Model translates into a pragmatic and forward-looking ethos: collaboration is not merely desirable—it is indispensable for sustained competitiveness and social relevance. Modern industries operate within complex ecosystems shaped by economic forces, cultural dynamics, technological innovation, and shifting societal expectations. The model therefore encourages enterprises to move beyond transactional relationships and embrace a co-creative posture with educational institutions, cultural sectors, government agencies, and philanthropic actors.

Industries that recognize the catalytic power of culture, creativity, and human talent are better positioned to innovate and adapt. The arts and creative industries, often underestimated in traditional economic frameworks, are in fact powerful engines of ideation, branding, design thinking, and cross-cultural communication. When industries engage with these sectors—whether through talent development, cultural partnerships, or creative problem-solving—they gain access to new forms of value creation that cannot be replicated through conventional economic inputs alone.

The model also underscores the importance of responsible industry leadership. Enterprises are encouraged to adopt a dual mandate:

- **Excellence in performance:** driven by innovation, efficiency, and market responsiveness; and
- **Commitment to societal well-being:** expressed through ethical governance, inclusive hiring, cultural engagement, and community investment.

This duality is not a burden; it is a strategic advantage. Industries that cultivate trust, cultural sensitivity, and social responsibility strengthen their brand legitimacy and resilience in an increasingly interconnected world. Moreover, by aligning with cultural practitioners, creative entrepreneurs, and philanthropic initiatives, industries contribute to social cohesion, talent mobility, and the broader socio-economic fabric of their nations.

In this sense, the Coadunate Economic Model positions industry not as an isolated economic actor, but as a co-architect of societal progress—a partner in shaping inclusive growth, cultural vitality, and sustainable development. It invites industries to recognize that their long-term success is inseparable from the well-being, creativity, and cultural richness of the societies in which they operate.

Relating the Model to Micro and Macro Economy in Modern Society:

The Coadunate Economic Model situates itself at the intersection of micro-level human agency and macro-level institutional design, asserting that modern economies thrive when these two spheres reinforce one another rather than operate in isolation. At the microeconomic level, the model emphasizes the empowerment of individuals, households, and small enterprises. It recognizes that economic vitality begins with people—their talents, their cultural expressions, their entrepreneurial capacities, and their sense of belonging within the social fabric. When citizens have access to opportunity, education, cultural participation, and creative expression, they contribute more dynamically to local markets and community development.

This micro-level strength is not merely economic; it is cultural and psychological. Cultural engagement reduces social fragmentation, enhances well-being, and fosters the confidence necessary for innovation and risk-taking. Creative entrepreneurs, artists, and cultural practitioners— often overlooked in traditional microeconomic analysis— play a pivotal role in shaping local economies through design, storytelling, performance, and cross-cultural communication. Their contributions ripple outward, influencing consumer behavior, community identity, and the vibrancy of local markets.

At the macroeconomic level, the Coadunate Model calls for harmonized policies that integrate economic planning with cultural development, social inclusion, and human capital formation. Macroeconomic stability—expressed through coherent fiscal policy, transparent governance, and strategic investment—creates the conditions in which micro-level actors can flourish. Yet the model goes further by asserting that culture itself is a macroeconomic asset. Cultural industries generate employment, stimulate innovation, attract tourism, and enhance a nation's global image. They contribute to GDP while simultaneously strengthening social cohesion and national resilience.

In a modern, multi-polar world, the relationship between micro and macro dynamics becomes even more critical. Global interdependence, technological acceleration, and demographic shifts require nations to cultivate both individual creativity and institutional coherence. The Coadunate Model bridges these realms by demonstrating that micro-level cultural vitality and macro-level policy alignment are mutually reinforcing. When individuals are empowered to create, participate, and innovate, they strengthen the broader economy. When national policies recognize and support cultural and creative sectors, they amplify the contributions of citizens and industries alike.

Thus, the model presents a holistic vision of economic life— one in which human creativity, cultural engagement, institutional alignment, and economic strategy operate in concert. It affirms that sustainable prosperity in modern society is not achieved through economic mechanisms alone, but through the deliberate integration of cultural, social, and economic forces at every level of national life.

Application for Developing and Emerging Economies:

For developing and emerging economies, the Coadunate Economic Model offers a practical and adaptable pathway toward coordinated national advancement. These nations often face the dual challenge of building institutional capacity while simultaneously expanding market participation and social inclusion. Fragmented approaches can slow progress; alignment accelerates it. The model therefore encourages governments, industries, cultural sectors, and civil society to move in concert, recognizing that sustainable development is achieved not through isolated interventions but through integrated, mutually reinforcing strategies.

Emerging economies possess a unique advantage: they are not bound by the rigid institutional legacies that characterize many mature systems. This flexibility allows them to adopt coadunate practices more readily—linking economic planning with cultural development, talent cultivation, and philanthropic engagement. When these elements are aligned, nations can generate new engines of growth rooted in creativity, innovation, and human potential.

A central premise of the model is that culture and the creative industries are not luxuries reserved for wealthy nations. They are powerful economic assets that can stimulate employment, foster entrepreneurship, and strengthen social cohesion. Creative entrepreneurs, artists, performers, and cultural practitioners contribute to local identity, tourism, design, digital innovation, and cross-cultural communication. Their work enhances a nation's global visibility and soft power, while also enriching domestic markets. When governments in developing contexts recognize and invest in this potential, they unlock new avenues for inclusive growth.

Moreover, the model underscores the importance of talent management and human capital development. Emerging economies often have young, dynamic populations whose creativity and adaptability can drive long-term transformation. By integrating cultural education, vocational training, and entrepreneurial support into national development strategies, these nations can cultivate a workforce capable of contributing to both traditional industries and the rapidly expanding creative economy.

Philanthropy also plays a catalytic role in this context. Strategic philanthropic initiatives—whether in education, cultural preservation, community development, or innovation—can fill critical gaps, support vulnerable populations, and accelerate social mobility. When philanthropy is aligned with public policy and industry priorities, it becomes a powerful lever for equitable development.

Ultimately, the Coadunate Economic Model provides developing and emerging economies with a framework that is both aspirational and actionable. It invites them to build systems that are culturally grounded, economically coherent, and socially inclusive. By embracing coadunation—by aligning institutions, industries, cultural sectors, and communities—these nations can chart development pathways that are resilient, innovative, and authentically their own.

Relation to Public Policy and Public Diplomacy:

Public policy, within the Coadunate Economic Model, is understood as an instrument of coherence—an architecture through which economic, cultural, social, and human-development priorities are aligned rather than pursued in isolation. Modern societies cannot afford fragmented policymaking; they require policies that reinforce one another and reflect the interconnected realities of a multi-polar world. The model therefore calls for integrated policy design, where economic planning is informed by cultural insight, social inclusion, talent development, and long-term national vision. In this context, culture is not an afterthought; it is a strategic policy domain. Cultural policy intersects with education, innovation, immigration, tourism, and community development. When governments recognize the economic and social value of the cultural and creative industries, they unlock new pathways for employment, entrepreneurship, and social cohesion. Policies that support cultural participation, creative entrepreneurship, and cross-cultural engagement strengthen the very foundations upon which inclusive and resilient economies are built.

The model also extends naturally into the realm of public diplomacy, where nations communicate their values, aspirations, and identity to the world. Public diplomacy is most effective when it is grounded in authenticity, cultural richness, and societal coherence. A nation that demonstrates internal alignment—between its industries, institutions, cultural sectors, and communities—projects credibility and partnership readiness on the global stage. In this sense, coadunation becomes both a domestic virtue and an international asset. Within this broader diplomatic landscape, Cultural Diplomacy holds a particularly vital role. It is through cultural exchange, artistic collaboration, and creative dialogue that nations build trust, reduce misunderstanding, and foster long-term relationships. Cultural Diplomacy humanizes international engagement; it allows nations to speak not only through policy statements but through their stories, their art, their heritage, and their people. It strengthens soft power, enhances global visibility, and contributes to peacebuilding by emphasizing shared humanity over political division.

The Coadunate Economic Model affirms that Cultural Diplomacy is not merely symbolic—it is economically and socially consequential. Cultural initiatives stimulate tourism, attract investment, support creative industries, and open channels for international cooperation. They also reinforce domestic cohesion by celebrating diversity and promoting intercultural understanding. When Cultural Diplomacy is aligned with national policy and economic strategy, it becomes a powerful tool for advancing both national interests and global well-being.

Ultimately, the model positions public policy and public diplomacy as complementary forces. Public policy shapes the internal coherence of a nation; public diplomacy communicates that coherence to the world. Cultural Diplomacy bridges the two—strengthening national identity at home while cultivating meaningful relationships abroad. Together, they form a coadunate framework through which nations can pursue sustainable development, cultural vitality, and constructive global engagement.

Relation to Societal Well-Being and Good Citizenship:

The Coadunate Economic Model is ultimately a human-centered framework. While it addresses institutions, industries, and policy structures, its deepest concern is the well-being of individuals and the quality of life within communities. A society flourishes when its citizens feel empowered, included, and connected to one another; when they have access not only to economic opportunity but also to cultural participation, creative expression, and a sense of shared purpose. In this regard, the model affirms that societal well-being is not a by-product of economic growth—it is one of its essential foundations.

Cultural engagement plays a pivotal role in this process. When people participate in cultural life—whether through the arts, heritage, creative industries, or community traditions—they experience belonging, identity, and emotional resilience. Cultural activities reduce social isolation, strengthen mental health, and foster empathy across diverse groups. They create spaces where individuals can express themselves, encounter new perspectives, and build bridges across cultural, linguistic, and generational divides. These are not intangible benefits; they are measurable contributors to social stability and human development.

Good citizenship, within the coadunate framework, extends beyond legal compliance or civic duty. It is expressed through active participation in the cultural, social, and economic life of the nation. Citizens who engage with their communities, support creative initiatives, respect diversity, and contribute to collective well-being embody the very principles that sustain a healthy society. Their actions reinforce social cohesion, strengthen democratic culture, and cultivate a shared sense of responsibility for the common good.

The model also recognizes that societal well-being is inseparable from fairness and inclusion. When individuals—regardless of background, ethnicity, or socio-economic status—have access to cultural resources, educational opportunities, and creative platforms, they are more likely to develop confidence, agency, and a sense of belonging. This, in turn, reduces social tensions and enhances national unity. A society that invests in its cultural and creative sectors invests in the emotional and psychological health of its people.

Moreover, the Coadunate Economic Model highlights the reciprocal relationship between citizens and institutions. Institutions that operate transparently, ethically, and in alignment with cultural and social values inspire trust and participation. Citizens who feel valued and represented are more inclined to contribute positively to public life. This mutual reinforcement—between engaged citizens and responsive institutions—is a hallmark of a coadunate society.

Ultimately, the model asserts that societal well-being and good citizenship are not peripheral ideals; they are central to national resilience and long-term prosperity. A society that nurtures creativity, cultural vitality, and human dignity builds the conditions for innovation, stability, and shared growth. In this sense, the Coadunate Economic Model offers not only an economic vision but a social and cultural one—affirming that the strength of a nation lies in the well-being, creativity, and active participation of its people.

Positive Outcomes and Promises for a Nation:

The Coadunate Economic Model offers nations a compelling promise: that sustainable prosperity emerges when economic strategy, cultural vitality, institutional coherence, and human creativity move in alignment. When these elements reinforce one another, a nation gains not only economic strength but also social resilience, cultural confidence, and diplomatic credibility. The model therefore presents a multidimensional vision of national advancement—one that is grounded in human dignity, cultural richness, and shared purpose.

One of the most significant outcomes of adopting a coadunate approach is institutional coherence. When public policy, industry strategy, cultural development, and social programs are aligned, nations reduce duplication, minimize policy contradictions, and enhance the effectiveness of governance. This coherence builds public trust and strengthens the social contract between citizens and institutions.

A second outcome is enhanced national competitiveness. Nations that invest in creativity, cultural industries, and talent development cultivate innovation ecosystems capable of responding to global challenges. Creative entrepreneurs, artists, designers, and cultural practitioners contribute to branding, tourism, digital innovation, and cross-cultural communication—areas that increasingly define global competitiveness in a multi-polar world.

The model also promises inclusive and human-centered growth. By recognizing the economic and social value of culture, nations can generate employment, stimulate local economies, and support vulnerable communities. Cultural participation fosters belonging, reduces social fragmentation, and strengthens mental and emotional well-being. These are not peripheral benefits; they are essential components of a stable and cohesive society.

Another key promise is greater national resilience. Nations that cultivate cultural vitality, social cohesion, and institutional alignment are better equipped to withstand economic shocks, demographic shifts, and geopolitical uncertainties. Cultural Diplomacy further enhances this resilience by strengthening international relationships, expanding soft power, and positioning the nation as a constructive global partner.

The Coadunate Economic Model also contributes to elevated global standing and diplomatic credibility. When a nation demonstrates internal harmony—between its industries, institutions, cultural sectors, and communities— it projects reliability and partnership readiness on the world stage. Cultural Diplomacy amplifies this effect by showcasing the nation's creativity, diversity, and humanistic values.

Finally, the model promises a more engaged, empowered, and culturally confident citizenry. When individuals have access to cultural resources, creative platforms, and opportunities for participation, they develop agency, empathy, and a sense of shared responsibility. Good citizenship flourishes in environments where people feel connected to their communities and confident in their cultural identity.

In essence, the Coadunate Economic Model offers nations a holistic pathway toward prosperity—one that integrates economic performance with cultural vitality, social inclusion, and global engagement. It affirms that the true strength of a nation lies not only in its markets or institutions, but in the creativity, well-being, and collective spirit of its people.

Closing Perspective:

The Coadunate Economic Model stands as a reminder that the strength of a nation is not measured solely by its markets or institutions, but by the coherence with which its economic, cultural, and human capacities are brought together. In an era defined by complexity and interdependence, fragmented approaches no longer suffice. Nations require frameworks that recognize the interplay between creativity and productivity, between cultural vitality and economic resilience, between individual agency and institutional design.

This model offers such a framework. It invites policymakers, industries, cultural practitioners, and citizens to see themselves as partners in a shared project of national development. It affirms that economic growth gains meaning when it uplifts communities; that cultural expression becomes transformative when it informs policy and diplomacy; and that citizenship flourishes when people feel connected to the cultural and social fabric of their society.

By embracing coadunation—by aligning systems, sectors, and human energies—nations can cultivate environments where innovation thrives, where diversity is celebrated, and where prosperity is both sustainable and inclusive. The promise of the Coadunate Economic Model is not merely a more efficient economy, but a more harmonious and humane society. It offers a vision of development rooted in dignity, creativity, and collective purpose—one that equips nations to navigate the challenges of a multi-polar world with confidence, clarity, and cultural depth.

Publisher's Affirmation:

The Coadunate Economic Model, conceived by Dr. Mosi Dorbayani (2005), has garnered distinguished recognition across both media and academic spheres. Forbes Journal and Tycoon Herald have referred to Dr. Dorbayani as *"The Father of the Coadunate Economic Model,"* underscoring his pioneering influence in advancing integrative economic thought. The University of Salford (UK) awarded him the world's first ever practice-based PhD in Cultural Diplomacy, with his thesis featuring this groundbreaking model—further affirming its scholarly and diplomatic significance.

These acknowledgments—together with features in Spotlight Magazine (Canada), The Ritz Herald (USA), JOISS Research (Canada), and various institutional profiles—attest to the model's growing impact on interdisciplinary discourse and its practical relevance within emerging policy frameworks.

Useful Links:

Dorbayani, Dr. Mosi (2022). The Coadunate Economic Model: WAALM and Cultural Diplomacy for Social Impact. University of Salford. Presentation. https://doi.org/10.17866/rd.salford.19492079.v1

Dorbayani, M. (n.d.). *Mosi Dorbayani – EverybodyWiki Bios & Wiki.* EverybodyWiki. https://en.everybodywiki.com/Mosi_Dorbayani

The Ritz Herald. (2025). *How the Canadian polymath views today's world*. The Ritz Herald. https://ritzherald.com/how-the-canadian-polymath-views-todays-world/

Tycoon Herald. (2021, February 24). *Meet the father of the Coadunate Economic Model*. https://tycoonherald.com/meet-the-father-of-the-coadunate-economic-model/

University of Salford, Dorbayani, Dr. Mosi (2022). The Coadunate Economic Model: WAALM and Cultural Diplomacy for Social Impact. University of Salford. Presentation. https://doi.org/10.17866/rd.salford.19492079.v1

"Trust is a bridge built not by grand gestures, but by the steady rhythm of reliability and care."

Mosi Dorbayani

Briefing 3.

THE GRAMMAR OF BELONGING: THE NEUROPSYCHOLOGICAL FOUNDATIONS OF TOGETHERNESS

In Brief:

Culture does not reside outside of us; it is not an ornament we wear, nor a script we merely recite. Culture lives through us—etched into the neural folds of our being, shaping how we feel, interpret, and respond to the world. The brain, in its remarkable plasticity, is not a passive observer of cultural life; it is an active architect, continuously sculpted by the rituals, symbols, and emotional climates that surround us.

From the earliest days of infancy, cultural signals arrive not as abstractions but as sensory rhythms: the cadence of a mother's voice, the communal patterns of touch, the emotional temperature of a household, the rituals that mark beginnings and endings. These experiences are encoded through neural pathways that bind emotion to meaning. What we later call "tradition" or "identity" is, in fact, a constellation of synaptic memories—engraved through repetition, reinforced through belonging, and animated by shared narratives.

The brain's limbic system, our emotional compass, is particularly sensitive to cultural cues. It learns what is safe, what is sacred, what is shameful, and what is celebrated. Over time, these emotional imprints become psychodynamic forces: they guide our motivations, shape our interpersonal expectations, and influence how we negotiate trust, conflict, and cooperation. Thus, culture becomes not only a social phenomenon but a neuropsychological one—an internalized map that directs our relational life.

Yet culture also speaks to the prefrontal cortex, the seat of reasoning and foresight. Through language, symbols, and collective memory, it teaches us how to interpret complexity, how to frame our aspirations, and how to imagine futures that extend beyond the self. In this way, cultural experience becomes a cognitive scaffold, enabling us to think with the wisdom of generations rather than the limitations of a single lifetime.

When we participate in music, ceremony, or shared storytelling, the brain synchronizes with others—literally aligning neural oscillations in moments of collective resonance. This is not poetic metaphor; it is measurable neuroscience. Culture binds us through biological harmony, reminding us that belonging is not merely emotional but physiological.

Thus, the encoding of cultural experience is both intimate and expansive. It shapes the individual psyche while simultaneously sustaining the social fabric. It is the quiet architect of our emotional lives and the unseen strategist of our collective behavior. To understand culture, then, is to understand the brain; and to understand the brain is to recognize that our humanity is, at its core, a shared and evolving cultural symphony.

When Emotional Imprints Evolve into Unconscious Drivers:

Emotional imprints formed within a cultural environment do not remain as isolated memories; they evolve into enduring psychodynamic forces that shape how individuals interpret and navigate their social world. Each repeated cultural cue—whether a gesture of respect, a ritual of belonging, or a collective response to conflict—creates a patterned emotional expectation within the psyche. Over time, these expectations crystallize into unconscious templates that guide how we anticipate others will behave, how we regulate our own emotions, and how we assign meaning to interpersonal events. What appears as "personality" or "temperament" is often the accumulated residue of these culturally mediated emotional lessons, encoded in neural circuits that privilege familiarity, coherence, and survival.

As these imprints deepen, they begin to influence not only personal behavior but also collective dynamics. They shape how communities negotiate trust, authority, and intimacy; how they respond to uncertainty; and how they construct narratives of identity and purpose. In this sense, psychodynamic forces are not merely intrapsychic—they are socio-cultural currents that flow through individuals, binding them to shared emotional grammars. When we understand these forces, we gain insight into why societies differ in their approaches to leadership, conflict, cooperation, and healing. The emotional past becomes the psychological present, and culture becomes a living architecture within the mind, continuously shaping the contours of human behavior.

Shared Emotional Grammars:

Socio-cultural currents move through individuals much like an undersea tide—quiet, persistent, and profoundly shaping. These currents are composed of the rituals, symbols, emotional norms, and collective memories that define a community's way of feeling and interpreting the world. As individuals absorb these patterns, they internalize not only the visible customs but also the subtle emotional codes that govern belonging, respect, conflict, and care. Over time, these codes become intuitive: we "feel" what is appropriate long before we consciously articulate it. In this way, culture becomes an emotional language—one learned through immersion rather than instruction.

These shared emotional grammars allow individuals to synchronize with one another, creating a sense of coherence and mutual intelligibility. They guide how communities express joy, navigate sorrow, respond to uncertainty, and construct meaning. Even when people believe they are acting independently, they are often moving in rhythm with these inherited emotional structures. The result is a collective emotional architecture that shapes not only interpersonal relationships but also institutions, leadership styles, and societal expectations. Through these currents, culture becomes more than a social environment—it becomes a living emotional ecosystem that flows through every individual, linking personal experience to the broader human story.

An Invisible Score:

Shared emotional grammars function like an invisible score that allows individuals to move in harmony, even without conscious coordination. When people grow within the same cultural-emotional environment, they learn similar cues for expressing warmth, signaling respect, navigating tension, or offering comfort. These cues become intuitive—embedded in tone, gesture, timing, and expectation. Because they are shared, individuals can anticipate one another's emotional rhythms, reduce friction and increase the ease of connection. This synchronization creates a felt sense of coherence: interactions "flow," misunderstandings lessen, and people experience a natural alignment in how they interpret and respond to the world.

This mutual intelligibility extends beyond interpersonal exchanges; it becomes the foundation of collective life. Communities that share emotional grammars can mobilize around common goals, respond cohesively to crises, and maintain social trust with greater stability. Leaders, institutions, and cultural rituals all rely on these grammars to communicate meaning in ways that resonate deeply and predictably. In this sense, emotional synchronization is not merely a social convenience—it is a cultural technology that sustains belonging, continuity, and the psychological architecture of community itself.

For example, imagine a community gathering for a seasonal celebration. No one instructs the children on when to laugh, when to clap, or how to show respect during the ceremonial moment—they simply absorb the emotional rhythm around them. The adults share a familiar tone of warmth, the pauses in conversation feel natural, and everyone seems to know when to shift from lively storytelling to quiet reflection. Even newcomers quickly sense the emotional flow and adjust their behavior without needing explicit guidance.

This is emotional grammar in action: people synchronize because they share an intuitive understanding of how to feel and respond together. The celebration "works" not because of rules written on paper, but because the community carries a shared emotional language that makes the gathering coherent, fluid, and mutually intelligible.

Neural Pathways of Collective Cohesion:

From a neuropsychological perspective, shared emotional grammars act as a kind of collective neural alignment system—an internalized set of emotional cues, expectations, and regulatory patterns that allow individuals within a community to coordinate their behavior with remarkable efficiency. When people share similar emotional templates, their brains process social signals in comparable ways: they interpret threat similarly, recognize safety similarly, and respond to leadership or collective calls to action with a shared emotional logic. This reduces cognitive load during moments of uncertainty because individuals do not need to decipher unfamiliar emotional cues; instead, they rely on well-established neural pathways shaped by cultural experience. The result is faster coordination, smoother communication, and a heightened capacity for unified action.

During crises, these shared emotional grammars become even more critical. Communities with aligned emotional processing exhibit more synchronized stress responses— meaning their collective neurobiology supports cohesion rather than fragmentation. Mirror-neuron systems, limbic resonance, and culturally conditioned regulatory strategies help individuals attune to one another, reinforcing trust and reducing panic. Over time, this neuropsychological synchrony strengthens social bonds and stabilizes group identity. Trust becomes not merely a social contract but a neurobiological expectation: the brain anticipates cooperation because it has repeatedly encoded it as the norm. In this way, emotional grammars serve as the neural infrastructure of social stability, enabling communities to mobilize, endure, and recover with greater resilience.

Below is a set of practices—both individual and community-level—that strengthen and diversify emotional grammars by enriching the brain's repertoire of cooperative, attuned, and culturally resonant emotional patterns. These are framed in a way that aligns with the neuropsychological logic you're developing.

Exercises That Cultivate a More Dynamic Emotional Grammar:

1. Individual Practices:

➤ Cross-Context Emotional Training:

Engaging in activities that expose the brain to varied emotional cues—such as learning a new language, participating in unfamiliar rituals, or practicing intercultural dialogue—broadens the neural templates for empathy and interpretation. The brain becomes more flexible in decoding emotional nuance, reducing rigid responses and increasing adaptive cooperation.

➢ Reflective Emotional Mapping:

Journaling or contemplative practice that identifies emotional triggers, cultural assumptions, and habitual responses helps individuals recognize the "grammar rules" they've internalized. This metacognitive awareness allows the brain to update old patterns and encode new, more constructive ones.

➢ Rhythmic Synchronization Activities:

Music, drumming, chanting, or coordinated movement (such as martial arts kata or group breathing) activate neural circuits involved in limbic resonance. These practices strengthen the brain's capacity for attunement, making cooperative responses more intuitive.

➢ Compassion and Perspective-Taking Exercises:

Guided imagery, narrative empathy (reading or listening to stories from different cultural perspectives), and structured gratitude practices enhance neural pathways associated with prosocial behavior. Over time, the brain encodes cooperation as emotionally rewarding.

2. Community Practices:

➤ Shared Rituals and Ceremonies:

Communities that engage in regular, meaningful rituals—seasonal gatherings, cultural celebrations, collective silence, or shared meals—reinforce synchronized emotional rhythms. These rituals act as "grammar lessons," teaching members how to feel together and respond cohesively.

➤ Collective Storytelling and Dialogue Circles:

Spaces where people share personal narratives, cultural memories, or intergenerational stories help align emotional interpretations across the group. The brain learns to anticipate cooperation because it repeatedly experiences emotional resonance in a communal setting.

➢ Collaborative Creative Projects:

Group music-making, mural painting, theatre, or community design projects activate neural networks for coordination, trust, and shared intention. These activities create a lived experience of cooperation, strengthening the emotional grammar of unity.

➢ Intercultural Exchange and Rotating Leadership:

When communities intentionally rotate roles, invite diverse voices, or engage in cross-cultural exchanges, they expand their collective emotional repertoire. The brain learns that cooperation is not tied to a single hierarchy or identity but is a flexible, shared capacity.

➢ Crisis Simulation and Collective Problem-Solving:

Low-stakes simulations—such as community planning exercises, emergency drills, or collaborative strategy workshops—train the brain to respond cohesively under pressure. These experiences encode resilience as a communal norm rather than an individual burden.

Why The Above Practices Work Neuropsychologically:

✓ They activate mirror-neuron systems, enhancing attunement.

✓ They reinforce limbic resonance, making emotional synchronization more natural.

✓ They expand neural plasticity, allowing new emotional patterns to form.

✓ They reward cooperation, strengthening prosocial circuits in the brain.

✓ They create predictable emotional environments, which the brain encodes as safe and trustworthy.

The Grand Architect of Emotional Grammar:

Public policy can act as the macro-level architect of emotional grammars—shaping the environments, incentives, and shared experiences that allow individuals and communities to develop richer, more adaptive emotional repertoires. When policy is designed with an understanding of neuropsychology, it becomes a tool for cultivating cooperation, resilience, and social trust. Here is how public policy decisions can strengthen the dynamic emotional grammar:

1. **Institutionalizing Shared Rituals and Collective Experiences:**

Policies that support cultural festivals, civic ceremonies, intergenerational gatherings, and community arts programs create predictable emotional rhythms that reinforce belonging. These shared experiences activate limbic resonance at scale, allowing communities to "feel together" and encode cooperation as a norm. When governments invest in cultural life, they are investing in the neural infrastructure of social cohesion.

2. **Embedding Emotional Literacy in Education Systems:**

Curricula that include emotional regulation, intercultural communication, reflective practice, and collaborative problem-solving help young people develop flexible emotional grammars early in life. Neuropsychologically, this strengthens prefrontal-limbic integration, making empathy, cooperation, and perspective-taking more automatic. Policy can mandate these competencies as core—not peripheral—skills.

3. Designing Public Spaces That Encourage Social Synchrony:

Urban planning and community design influence how often people encounter one another, how safe they feel, and how easily they can engage in shared activities. Parks, plazas, libraries, and cultural centers serve as neural meeting grounds where emotional grammars are practiced and reinforced. Policy that prioritizes inclusive, accessible public space fosters spontaneous social attunement.

4. Supporting Intercultural Exchange and Rotating Leadership Models:

Policies that encourage cross-cultural dialogue, exchange programs, and participatory governance expose communities to diverse emotional cues. This broadens the collective emotional repertoire and reduces rigid in-group patterns. Neuropsychologically, such exposure enhances cognitive flexibility and reduces threat responses to difference.

5. Funding Community-Based Arts, Music, and Movement Programs:

Music, dance, theatre, and coordinated movement are powerful synchronizers of neural activity. When policy supports these programs—especially in schools, community centers, and public health initiatives—it strengthens the brain's capacity for attunement and collective regulation. These activities literally train the nervous system for cooperation.

6. Integrating Collective Problem-Solving into Governance:

Public consultations, participatory budgeting, and community planning exercises allow citizens to practice collaborative decision-making. These experiences encode cooperation as a lived norm rather than an abstract ideal. Over time, they build neural pathways that associate civic engagement with agency, trust, and shared purpose.

7. Ensuring Stability, Predictability, and Fairness in Institutions:

The brain thrives on predictability. When institutions behave consistently and transparently, they reduce collective stress responses and strengthen trust. Policies that uphold procedural fairness, clear communication, and reliable social safety nets create emotional environments where cooperation feels safe and natural.

The Neuropsychological Logic Behind Policy's Role:

Public policy shapes the emotional ecosystem in which neural patterns form.

It influences:

- ➢ What emotions are repeatedly reinforced
- ➢ How communities synchronize their responses
- ➢ Which behaviors are rewarded or discouraged
- ➢ How safe people feel when engaging with others
- ➢ Whether cooperation becomes a default or a risk

In essence, policy is not only administrative—it is emotional architecture. It builds the conditions under which dynamic, resilient emotional grammars can flourish.

In closing, the thread that runs through every layer of this exploration is simple yet profound: human resilience is not an individual trait but a shared neurological achievement. When emotional grammars are nurtured—through culture, community, and thoughtful public policy—the brain learns to anticipate cooperation, not conflict; connection, not withdrawal. We become more capable together than we ever could alone. Strengthening these shared emotional patterns is, ultimately, an investment in the collective mind of a society: its capacity to mobilize with clarity, to endure with dignity, and to recover with a sense of purpose that is both personal and communal.

Briefing 4.

THE NEUROPSYCHOLOGY OF CIVIC HEALTH

In Brief:

Human beings are social organisms whose brains were shaped by relationships long before institutions existed. At the neural level, social interactions recruit circuits for reward, threat detection, memory, and meaning-making: the mesolimbic pathways that encode social reward, the amygdala and insula that signal social threat and pain, and the prefrontal networks that regulate impulse, perspective-taking, and moral judgment. These circuits do not operate in isolation; they are sculpted by culture, history, and policy. When public policy and cultural diplomacy attend to the neurobiology of belonging, they become instruments not only of governance but of civic health.

With the above in mind, the mesolimbic system—centered on dopamine-rich projections between the ventral tegmental area and the nucleus accumbens—translates social affirmation into motivational energy, reinforcing cooperative behaviors and civic participation. Simultaneously, the amygdala and insula act as rapid detectors of social threat, amplifying vigilance when cues signal exclusion, injustice, or symbolic denigration. The prefrontal cortex integrates these signals over time, enabling perspective-taking, impulse control, and the moral reasoning necessary for deliberative democracy. These neural dynamics are continuously modulated by developmental experiences, socioeconomic conditions, and cultural narratives; early attachment patterns and chronic stressors calibrate baseline reactivity, while public narratives and institutional practices shape which social cues are interpreted as rewarding or threatening. Because these systems are plastic, policy choices exert measurable neurobiological effects. Policies that reduce unpredictability—through reliable social services, transparent decision-making, and equitable access to resources—lower chronic stress and preserve prefrontal capacity for complex reasoning. Conversely, policies that stigmatize or marginalize groups heighten amygdala-driven threat responses and narrow attentional bandwidth, making collective problem-solving more difficult. Cultural diplomacy that foregrounds shared narratives and mutual recognition can engage mirror and mentalizing networks, softening defensive postures and creating neural conditions conducive to empathy and reciprocity. In this sense, governance that is attuned to neural and psychological realities does more than manage populations; it cultivates the cognitive and affective infrastructure of civic life.

Translating these insights into practice requires interventions at multiple timescales: early childhood programs that support secure attachment and executive function; urban design and public services that reduce cognitive load and unpredictability in daily life; and cultural exchanges that intentionally humanize difference and repair symbolic harms.

Evaluation should pair behavioral and participation metrics with biomarkers of stress and resilience to capture both subjective meaning and physiological impact. Ethically, such an approach demands humility—recognizing the limits of reductionism—and a commitment to dignity, ensuring that neuro-informed policies empower rather than instrumentalize citizens.

Civic Health:

Civic health is the emergent property of individuals who feel seen, safe, and efficacious within a polity. Neuroscience shows that social exclusion and chronic uncertainty produce sustained activation of stress systems, impairing executive function and narrowing attention. Conversely, predictable institutions and inclusive cultural narratives reduce allostatic load and free cognitive resources for deliberation and cooperation. Public policy that reduces unpredictability — through stable social safety nets, transparent processes, and equitable access to services — functions neurobiologically as a scaffold for higher-order civic capacities: deliberative reasoning, empathy, and sustained civic engagement.

When people experience their civic environment as coherent and trustworthy, the brain's regulatory systems shift from defensive vigilance to exploratory engagement. The prefrontal cortex, freed from the metabolic drag of chronic stress, can sustain the cognitive flexibility required for pluralistic dialogue and long-term planning. This is not merely an individual benefit; it becomes a collective asset. Communities with lower allostatic load demonstrate higher levels of cooperation, greater tolerance for ambiguity, and stronger norms of reciprocity. In this sense, civic health is not a metaphor but a measurable psychophysiological condition shaped by the design of public life.

Cultural diplomacy plays a parallel role by shaping the symbolic environment in which neural interpretations of "us" and "them" are formed. Narratives that affirm shared dignity and mutual recognition activate neural circuits associated with social reward and perspective-taking, while narratives of humiliation or exclusion amplify threat responses and entrench defensive postures. When cultural diplomacy foregrounds interdependence, it helps recalibrate the social brain toward openness rather than suspicion. This is why rituals of recognition, cross-cultural exchange, and public storytelling are not peripheral to governance; they are mechanisms through which societies regulate collective emotional tone and reduce the neurobiological precursors of polarization.

Ultimately, civic health emerges from the interplay between institutional design, cultural meaning, and the neural architecture of human sociality. Policies that stabilize daily life, narratives that humanize difference, and institutions that reliably honor procedural fairness all converge to create a civic ecosystem in which individuals can think clearly, relate generously, and participate meaningfully. When these conditions are met, the polity becomes more than a structure of rules; it becomes a psychologically sustainable habitat for democratic life.

Cultural Diplomacy for Social Cohesion:

Cultural diplomacy operates at the level of narrative and symbol, shaping the stories that communities tell about themselves and others. Narratives that humanize difference engage mirror and mentalizing systems, facilitating perspective-taking and attenuating threat responses. Rituals of recognition, whether local commemorations or international cultural exchanges, activate reward circuits tied to social cohesion.

Thoughtful cultural diplomacy can therefore be read as a form of neural hygiene: it cultivates patterns of attention and valuation that make cooperation more likely and polarization less durable.

When cultural diplomacy is practiced with psychological sophistication, it becomes a way of tending to the collective nervous system. Symbols, ceremonies, and shared artistic experiences provide predictable social cues that help regulate affect and reduce the cognitive load associated with uncertainty.

In moments of social strain, these shared cultural anchors can interrupt cycles of reactivity by reminding communities of their interdependence and their capacity for mutual regard.

Neuroscience shows that such reminders are not merely sentimental; they recalibrate neural networks involved in trust, empathy, and social prediction. In this sense, cultural diplomacy is a stabilizing force that helps societies maintain coherence even amid rapid change.

At the same time, cultural diplomacy can serve as a corrective to historical distortions and inherited biases. When institutions elevate marginalized voices, revise public narratives, or create spaces for reciprocal cultural exchange, they invite the brain to update entrenched threat associations and expand its repertoire of social understanding.

This process is slow, but it is measurable: repeated exposure to dignifying representations of difference strengthens neural pathways associated with curiosity rather than fear. Over time, these shifts accumulate into broader patterns of civic behavior—greater willingness to collaborate, reduced susceptibility to dehumanizing rhetoric, and a more resilient sense of shared fate.

Ultimately, cultural diplomacy for social cohesion is not an ornamental supplement to policy but a foundational component of civic health. It shapes the emotional climate in which laws are interpreted, institutions are trusted, and collective decisions are made. By aligning symbolic life with the neurobiological conditions that support empathy and cooperation, cultural diplomacy helps build a polity capable of sustaining democratic life not only in principle but in practice.

Psychodynamics of Civic Health:

Psychodynamics offers a bridge between individual interiority and collective life. Unconscious anxieties, projection, and group-level defenses are not merely metaphors; they have measurable correlates in attention, memory bias, and threat sensitivity. Policies that ignore these dynamics — for example, punitive measures that stigmatize vulnerable groups — amplify defensive neural states and entrench social fragmentation. By contrast, policies that acknowledge trauma, repair harm, and create avenues for meaningful participation modulate neural systems toward trust and openness. Reparative justice, restorative practices, and participatory policymaking are therefore not only ethical choices but neurobiological interventions. Implementation requires humility and interdisciplinarity. Neuroscience should inform policy without reducing citizens to circuits; psychodynamics should illuminate motives without excusing harm. Practical steps include designing civic spaces that lower cognitive load (clear signage, predictable procedures), investing in early childhood programs that foster secure attachment and executive function, and supporting cultural exchanges that foreground shared human concerns rather than exoticism.

Evaluation must combine quantitative metrics (stress biomarkers, participation rates) with qualitative accounts of meaning and dignity. Unconscious anxieties, projection, and group-level defenses are not merely metaphors; they have measurable correlates in attention, memory bias, and threat sensitivity. Policies that ignore these dynamics — for example, punitive measures that stigmatize vulnerable groups — amplify defensive neural states and entrench social fragmentation. By contrast, policies that acknowledge trauma, repair harm, and create avenues for meaningful participation modulate neural systems toward trust and openness. Reparative justice, restorative practices, and participatory policymaking are therefore not only ethical choices but neurobiological interventions.

When a society fails to metabolize its collective anxieties, those unprocessed tensions often reappear as political rigidity, scapegoating, or cycles of punitive governance. Psychodynamically, these are forms of group defense: attempts to manage fear by displacing it onto an "other," or by clinging to rigid structures that promise certainty. Neuroscience mirrors this pattern: heightened amygdala activation, reduced prefrontal integration, and a narrowing of attentional scope. Policies that rely on coercion or humiliation inadvertently reinforce these neural signatures, making it harder for communities to imagine alternatives or engage in cooperative problem-solving. In contrast, civic processes that invite reflection, dialogue, and shared authorship help diffuse these defensive patterns and restore a sense of agency.

Civic health deepens when institutions recognize that citizens are not only rational actors but emotional and relational beings. Psychodynamic literacy allows policymakers to anticipate how shame, loss, or historical trauma may shape public responses to reform. It also highlights the importance of symbolic gestures — apologies, acknowledgments, inclusive rituals — which can reduce collective defensiveness and reopen neural pathways associated with curiosity and connection. When people feel that their experiences are named rather than denied, the nervous system shifts from vigilance to engagement, creating the psychological spaciousness necessary for democratic participation.

Implementation requires humility and interdisciplinarity. Neuroscience should inform policy without reducing citizens to circuits; psychodynamics should illuminate motives without excusing harm. Practical steps include designing civic spaces that lower cognitive load (clear signage, predictable procedures), investing in early childhood programs that foster secure attachment and executive function, and supporting cultural exchanges that foreground shared human concerns rather than exoticism. Evaluation must combine quantitative metrics (stress biomarkers, participation rates) with qualitative accounts of meaning and dignity.

Taken together, a psychodynamically informed approach to civic health reframes governance as a relational practice. It recognizes that institutions shape not only material conditions but also the emotional climate in which civic life unfolds. By integrating insights from mind, brain, and culture, policymakers can cultivate environments where trust becomes possible, cooperation becomes sustainable, and democratic life becomes psychologically livable.

Ethical Imperative:

The ethical imperative is clear: civic health demands policies that honor human complexity. When governance integrates insights from brain science and psychodynamic thought, it can craft environments where citizens are not merely managed but enabled to flourish. Cultural diplomacy, when practiced with psychological sophistication, becomes a tool for healing as much as for influence. The task for leaders, scholars, and practitioners is to translate these insights into institutions that respect vulnerability, cultivate trust, and sustain the neural and social conditions for democratic life.

This ethical horizon also requires a shift in how societies understand responsibility. Instead of framing civic challenges as failures of individual willpower or moral character, a neuro-psychodynamic lens reveals how structural conditions shape attention, emotion, and behavior. Chronic stress, social humiliation, and institutional unpredictability are not abstractions; they alter neural pathways and reinforce defensive social postures. Ethical governance therefore begins with the recognition that dignity is not a luxury but a precondition for cognitive clarity and civic participation. Policies that reduce shame, stabilize daily life, and affirm belonging are not indulgent—they are foundational to democratic capacity.

Equally important is the commitment to designing institutions that can metabolize conflict without collapsing into polarization. Ethical leadership acknowledges that disagreement is inevitable, but dehumanization is not. When institutions create structured spaces for dialogue, repair, and shared authorship, they help communities process collective anxieties rather than displace them onto scapegoats. This is where ethics, neuroscience, and psychodynamics converge: they all point toward the same truth—that societies flourish when they cultivate environments in which people can regulate emotion, tolerate complexity, and remain open to one another. In this light, the ethical imperative is not simply to avoid harm, but to actively build the psychological and cultural infrastructure that allows democratic life to endure.

In Closing:

Taken together, these perspectives reveal that civic health is not an abstract ideal but a living system shaped by the interplay of neural regulation, cultural meaning, and institutional design. A society thrives when its structures reduce unnecessary threat, its narratives affirm shared dignity, and its policies create predictable conditions in which people can think, relate, and participate with openness rather than fear. When leaders recognize that human beings are biologically and psychologically interdependent, governance shifts from managing populations to cultivating the conditions in which collective intelligence can emerge.

This integrated approach also reframes democracy as a relational achievement rather than a procedural formality. The vitality of a polity depends on its ability to metabolize conflict, repair harm, and sustain a symbolic environment in which all members can recognize themselves as legitimate participants in the shared project of public life. Neuroscience underscores the fragility of this achievement; psychodynamics illuminates the forces that can undermine it; cultural diplomacy offers tools for renewing it. The ethical task, then, is to build institutions capable of holding complexity without collapsing into coercion or fragmentation.

Ultimately, civic health is a measure of how well a society understands itself—its vulnerabilities, its aspirations, and its profound interdependence. Policies grounded in this understanding do more than solve problems; they strengthen the neural and cultural foundations of democratic resilience. In an era marked by rapid change and collective strain, such an approach is not merely desirable but necessary.

"Your every 'Yes' or 'No', has a cost. Just make sure they don't cost your well-being."

Mosi Dorbayani

Briefing 5.

THE PSYCHOLOGICAL IMPACT OF AUTOMATION ON TEAMS: NEUROSCIENCE AT THE CROSSROADS OF PROGRESS AND PURPOSE

In Brief:

In every era of organizational evolution, humanity has stood at a crossroads between progress and purpose. Today, as automation reshapes the workplace, the question is no longer whether machines can perform tasks better or faster; the deeper question is how this transformation touches the human spirit within our teams. Automation, while promising efficiency, quietly introduces a psychological undercurrent that leaders must not ignore. When algorithms take over routine functions, employees often experience a subtle erosion of identity. Work has long been a source of meaning, contribution, and self-worth. When parts of that work are delegated to machines, individuals may begin to wonder: Where do I fit? What remains uniquely mine?

This is not resistance to technology—it is a natural human response to uncertainty. Teams may feel a collective sense of displacement, a fear that their relevance is diminishing. If left unaddressed, this can manifest as disengagement, anxiety, or a silent withdrawal from creative initiative.

Yet, within this challenge lies an extraordinary opportunity.

Automation can liberate teams from mechanical tasks and open space for deeper thinking, richer collaboration, and more purposeful engagement. But this shift does not happen automatically; it requires leaders who understand the psychology of transition. Leaders must reaffirm the irreplaceable value of human judgment, empathy, intuition, and ethical discernment—qualities no machine can replicate. When leaders communicate transparently, involve teams in shaping the future, and cultivate a culture where technology is seen as an ally rather than a threat, the psychological burden transforms into empowerment. Teams begin to see automation not as a competitor, but as a companion that amplifies their strengths.

Ultimately, the true impact of automation is not measured by productivity metrics alone, but by the emotional climate it creates. The organizations that will thrive are those that honor the human journey through technological change— those that recognize that progress is most sustainable when it elevates people, not when it replaces them.

As organizations navigate this turning point, the responsibility is not merely to implement new technologies, but to steward the emotional and cognitive well-being of the people who must live and work alongside them. The future will belong to leaders who understand that progress without purpose is hollow, and that the true measure of innovation lies in its ability to strengthen—not diminish—the human experience at the heart of every team.

Neuropsychology at the Crossroads of Progress and Purpose:

Neuropsychology teaches us that human beings are not merely processors of information; we are meaning-seeking organisms. Our brains are wired to interpret change not only through logic, but through emotion, identity, and a deep instinct for coherence. This is precisely where the author places emphasis on purpose, self-worth, and human dignity intersects with scientific insight.

In organizational life, this means that technological progress must be introduced with an understanding of how the mind constructs meaning—because when people can locate themselves within the story of change, they adapt with far greater confidence, resilience, and engagement.

1. The Brain's Need for Predictability and Purpose

Neuropsychological research shows that the human brain thrives on patterns. Predictability reduces cognitive load and creates a sense of safety. When progress—especially technological progress—disrupts familiar patterns, the brain interprets it as a potential threat.

> ➤ The amygdala becomes more active in uncertain environments.
> ➤ The prefrontal cortex, responsible for planning and meaning-making, works harder to re-establish coherence.

This is why individuals often feel unsettled at moments of rapid innovation. It is not resistance to progress; it is the brain's attempt to protect one's sense of identity and purpose.

The author yet gain highlights, *"people do not fear change; they fear losing themselves in the process."* Neuropsychology validates this sentiment.

2. Progress Without Purpose Creates Cognitive Dissonance

When technological advancement accelerates faster than human adaptation, the brain experiences a mismatch between:

- ➢ External progress (automation, new systems, new expectations)
- ➢ Internal purpose (identity, contribution, meaning)

This mismatch—known as cognitive dissonance—creates emotional friction. Individuals may feel:

- Displaced;
- Undervalued;
- Uncertain about their future role; and
- Disconnected from their sense of contribution.

With the above in mind, the author highlights that *purpose is not a luxury; it is a psychological necessity*. Neuropsychology confirms that purpose activates reward pathways, enhances resilience, and stabilizes emotional well-being.

3. The Human Brain Seeks Agency, Not Automation

Automation can unintentionally diminish a person's sense of agency—the feeling that one's actions matter. Neuropsychology shows that agency is tied to:

- Motivation;
- Creativity;
- Emotional stability; and
- Self-esteem.

When tasks are automated without a narrative that reinforces human value, the brain may interpret it as a loss of control. This is why Dorbayani emphasizes leadership that "restores the human place in the equation."

A deeper neuropsychological view reveals that agency is not merely a preference—it is a core component of how the brain maintains equilibrium. When individuals feel they no longer influence outcomes, the brain's reward circuitry becomes less active, reducing intrinsic motivation and weakening the sense of personal efficacy (Deci & Ryan, 2017). Over time, this can lead to disengagement or a quiet withdrawal from creative initiative. Leaders who intentionally preserve agency—by involving teams in decisions, clarifying the purpose behind automation, and highlighting the irreplaceable human elements of work—help re-activate these reward pathways. In doing so, they transform technological change from a perceived threat into an opportunity for renewed ownership, contribution, and psychological resilience.

4. Meaning-Making Is a Neuropsychological Imperative

The brain is constantly constructing stories to make sense of the world. When organizations introduce new technologies without a human-centered narrative, employees struggle to integrate the change into their personal story.

Hence, through his writings, the author often calls for leaders to be *"architects of meaning."* Neuropsychology supports this: meaning-making reduces stress, increases cognitive flexibility, and helps individuals embrace change with confidence rather than fear.

A growing body of research shows that when individuals cannot situate change within a coherent personal narrative, the brain interprets the disruption as a threat, activating stress responses and narrowing cognitive bandwidth (Park & George, 2018). Conversely, when leaders provide a clear, human-centered story that explains why change is happening and how people still matter within it, employees experience greater psychological stability and a renewed sense of relevance. This narrative coherence strengthens resilience, supports adaptive thinking, and allows teams to approach technological transitions with curiosity rather than apprehension.

5. Progress Becomes Sustainable Only When It Honors Human Psychology

Neuropsychology does not oppose progress; it simply reminds us that progress must be metabolized by the human mind. When leaders align innovation with purpose, they activate:

- The brain's reward system;
- Intrinsic motivation;

- Emotional engagement; and,
- Long-term adaptability.

This is precisely the crossroads the author often emphasises: *the meeting point where technological advancement must be guided by human wisdom.*

Research shows that when technological change is framed within a meaningful, human-centered context, the brain is more likely to interpret it as an opportunity rather than a threat. Meaningful framing activates neural pathways associated with reward, curiosity, and adaptive learning, enabling individuals to integrate new tools with greater psychological ease (Heath & Heath, 2020). Conversely, when innovation is introduced without purpose or narrative coherence, the brain's threat-detection systems become more active, narrowing attention and reducing openness to change. Leaders who intentionally connect progress with purpose help teams maintain cognitive flexibility, emotional stability, and a sense of shared direction—conditions essential for thriving in an era of rapid automation.

How Firms and Individuals Can Balance Progress and Purpose:

Below is a balanced, human-centric explanation—grounded in what psychology and organizational science actually tell us about preventing anxiety, stress, and mental-health strain in times of rapid progress.

As the author emphasises on dignity, meaning, and human leadership, in his view, progress becomes destabilizing only when it outpaces the human capacity to integrate it. Purpose is the stabilizer. When organizations honor both, they create environments where innovation uplifts rather than overwhelms. Here's how both firms and individuals can get this balance right:

For Firms: Building Cultures Where Progress Serves People

1. Anchor Innovation in a Human Narrative:

People don't fear new tools; they fear becoming irrelevant.

Organizations must articulate why progress matters and how it elevates human contribution.

- ✓ Explain how automation frees time for creativity and judgment;
- ✓ Reinforce the unique value of human insight and ethical reasoning; and,
- ✓ Share stories of employees who grew through technological change.

A narrative of inclusion reduces anxiety more effectively than any technical training.

2. Involve Employees in the Change Process:

Neuropsychology shows that agency reduces stress.

When employees help shape the future, they feel less threatened by it.

- ✓ Invite teams to co-design workflows;
- ✓ Ask for feedback before implementing new systems; and,
- ✓ Give people influence over how technology is integrated.

Note that, participation transforms fear into ownership.

3. Protect Psychological Safety During Transitions:

Rapid progress can trigger uncertainty, which activates stress responses.

Leaders must create climates where questions, concerns, and doubts are welcomed.

✓ Normalize learning curves
✓ Encourage open dialogue about fears
✓ Avoid framing automation as a competition

Remember that, psychological safety is the antidote to silent anxiety.

4. Redefine Roles Around Human Strengths

Instead of asking "What can machines do?", ask:

"What should humans always own?"

✓ Empathy;
✓ Ethical judgment;
✓ Creativity;
✓ Relationship-building; and,
✓ Complex decision-making.

When roles are redesigned around these strengths, purpose becomes self-evident.

5. Invest in Well-Being as a Strategic Priority:

Stress is not a personal weakness; it is a systemic signal.

Organizations that thrive treat well-being as infrastructure.

✓ Offer mental-health support;
✓ Build restorative rhythms into work;
✓ Train leaders in emotional intelligence; and,
✓ Encourage boundaries and recovery time.

Consider that, *progress without well-being is not progress—it's erosion.*

For Individuals: Staying Grounded in Times of Change

1. Reconnect With Your Core Purpose

When external change accelerates, internal clarity becomes essential.

Ask yourself:

✓ What values guide my work?

✓ What strengths do I bring that no machine can replicate?

✓ What kind of contribution gives me meaning?

Note that, purpose is a psychological anchor.

2. Cultivate Adaptability as a Skill, Not a Trait

Adaptability is not innate—it's practiced.

✓ Learn continuously,

✓ Stay curious, and,

✓ Treat new tools as opportunities to expand your identity.

Remember that, growth reduces fear.

3. Build Emotional Resilience

Resilience is strengthened through habits, not heroics.

✓ Maintain healthy routines,

✓ Seek supportive relationships,

✓ Practice reflection or mindfulness, and,

✓ Set boundaries around work.

A regulated mind navigates change with clarity.

4. Claim Your Human Advantages

Technology may outperform humans in speed, but not in humanity.

Lean into:

✓ Empathy;

✓ Intuition;

✓ Creativity;

✓ Moral reasoning; and,

✓ Interpersonal connection

These are perhaps your irreplaceable assets.

5. Ask for Support Early

Stress becomes harmful when carried alone.

Reaching out is not a sign of weakness—it's a sign of wisdom.

Speak with:

✓ Colleagues;

- ✓ Mentors;
- ✓ Friends; and,
- ✓ Mental-health professionals

Note that, human connection is a protective factor.

The Balance in One Sentence:

Progress must elevate human purpose, not eclipse it.

When organizations and individuals honor this principle, innovation becomes a source of empowerment rather than anxiety.

The psychological research reinforces this balance, showing that when technological advancement is paired with a clear sense of meaning, individuals experience greater resilience, motivation, and emotional stability (Steger, 2017). Purpose acts as a cognitive anchor, helping the brain interpret change as aligned with one's identity rather than a threat to it. In organizational settings, this means that progress is most sustainable when it strengthens the human experience—when innovation is introduced not as a replacement for people, but as a partner that amplifies their strengths, values, and contributions.

To that end, organizations may use and benefit for the policy sample in **appendix 1**.

In Closing:

In every period of technological transformation, organizations face a choice: to pursue progress as a purely mechanical upgrade, or to guide it as a human journey. Automation may streamline tasks, but its deeper impact is psychological—reshaping identity, agency, and the emotional architecture of work. Neuropsychology reminds us that people do not resist innovation itself; they resist losing the meaning, coherence, and sense of self that work has long provided. When change accelerates faster than the mind can integrate it, uncertainty becomes a silent burden.

Yet this moment also carries profound possibility. When leaders frame progress through a human-centered narrative—one that affirms purpose, dignity, and the irreplaceable value of human judgment—automation becomes an ally rather than a threat. Teams regain agency when they are invited into the process, supported through transition, and anchored in roles that elevate uniquely human strengths. In such environments, the brain's need for predictability, meaning, and contribution is not disrupted but renewed. Progress becomes a catalyst for creativity, collaboration, and deeper engagement.

The organizations that will thrive are those that understand that innovation is not only a technical shift but a psychological one. Sustainable progress emerges when firms honor the emotional realities of change and individuals reconnect with their core purpose. At this crossroads of progress and purpose, the true measure of leadership is not how efficiently technology is deployed, but how effectively the human experience is strengthened.

Appendix 1: Policy Sample

Note for Organizational Psychology Scholars and Students:

The following policy sample reflects the core insights of the briefing and serves as a practical model for applying change management and human-centered leadership in organizational settings. It demonstrates how firms can balance technological progress with psychological well-being—an essential competency for emerging professionals in Organizational Psychology. While you may use this model to develop your own policy, additional details may be required after consultation with your human resources department and executive leadership.

Organizational Policy on Human-Centered Integration of Automation

Ensuring Progress with Purpose, Dignity, and Psychological Well-Being.

1. Purpose of the Policy:

This policy establishes the organization's commitment to integrating automation in ways that protect and enhance the psychological well-being, identity, and agency of all employees. It ensures that technological progress aligns with human purpose, ethical leadership, and a culture of respect.

2. Guiding Principles:

Human First: Automation must elevate human contribution, not diminish it.

- Transparency: Employees will be informed early and clearly about technological changes.
- Psychological Safety: Questions, concerns, and uncertainties are welcomed without judgment.
- Agency and Participation: Employees will have meaningful opportunities to shape how automation is implemented.
- Purpose and Meaning: Work redesign must reinforce the unique value of human strengths—judgment, empathy, creativity, and ethical reasoning.

3. Communication Standards:

- Leaders must communicate the why behind automation, emphasizing how it supports human roles.

- All automation initiatives must include a narrative that reinforces employee relevance and contribution.
- Updates must be timely, accessible, and framed to reduce uncertainty.

4. Employee Involvement:

- Teams will be invited to co-design workflows affected by automation.
- Feedback loops will be built into every stage of technological transition.
- Employees may recommend adjustments to ensure tools support—not hinder—meaningful work.

5. Role Redesign and Human Strengths:

- Roles will be reviewed to ensure that uniquely human capabilities remain central.
- Automation will be used to remove mechanical or repetitive tasks, freeing employees for higher-value work.

- Leaders must highlight and protect the human elements essential to each role.

6. **Psychological Well-Being and Support:**

- The organization will provide resources that support emotional and cognitive adaptation during transitions.
- Leaders will be trained in emotional intelligence and change psychology.
- Workload, stress indicators, and team climate will be monitored to prevent burnout or disengagement.

7. **Learning and Adaptability:**

- Continuous learning is a shared expectation and will be supported through training and development.
- Employees will be encouraged to build new skills and explore expanded roles created by automation.
- Adaptability will be recognized as a developmental process, not an innate trait.

8. Accountability:

- Leaders are responsible for modeling human-centered integration of technology.
- Teams are responsible for engaging openly and constructively with new tools.
- The organization will review this policy annually to ensure alignment with evolving technologies and workforce needs.

References:

Deci, E. L., & Ryan, R. M. (2017). Self-determination theory: Basic psychological needs in motivation, development, and wellness. Guilford Press.

Heath, C., & Heath, D. (2020). Upstream: The quest to solve problems before they happen. Random House.

Park, C. L., & George, L. S. (2018). Meaning in life and meaning-making in the context of stressful life events: A psychological perspective. Journal of Health Psychology, 23(1), 25–35.

Steger, M. F. (2017). Creating meaning and purpose at work. In The Wiley Blackwell handbook of the psychology of positivity and strengths-based approaches at work (pp. 60–81). Wiley.

Briefing 6.

WHERE LAW LIVES IN CULTURE

In Brief:

Standing at the intersection where law meets culture, I am reminded that my own intellectual journey has always been a crossing of paths rather than a single, linear road. My studies in International Law, Economics, and Cultural Diplomacy prepared the ground beneath my feet, yet it was my practice as an executive adviser—and my lifelong devotion to the arts, to songwriting, to the human spirit—that compelled me to write this cross-disciplinary reflection. I have long believed that law and culture can be spoken in one breath. Their vocabularies may differ, their enforcement mechanisms may diverge, but their purpose remains shared: to cultivate order, to enable coexistence, and to safeguard the fragile harmony of human life.

International Law today is no longer the exclusive domain of states. It is invoked by individuals, corporations, activists, and international institutions alike. Environmental advocates scrutinize state behavior against global commitments; corporate lawyers navigate the tension between domestic regulations and international obligations; jurists and scholars increasingly recognize that no legal actor can afford to ignore the international dimension. Yet, even as law expands its reach, justice itself remains culturally interpreted. Every society carries its own legal culture—rooted in its traditions, shaped by its collective memory, and expressed through its unique understanding of codes, norms, and the role of law.

For this reason, dialogue among those who interpret, enact, and enforce laws is not merely beneficial; it is indispensable. Cultural differences and legal traditions are not obstacles to be overcome but realities to be understood. Without a clear appreciation of local culture, no assessment of law—its purpose, its legitimacy, its impact—can be complete. Studying the cultural roots of law is not an academic luxury; it is a practical necessity for achieving harmony. And harmony, I would argue, should be the guiding value for all who engage with International Law or Customary Law.

We are living through a profound redistribution of global power. New economic actors are emerging. Brexit has reshaped regional alliances. Nationalism has resurfaced across continents. New partnerships—China-Russia, the

South America Community of Nations, and others—are challenging long-standing geopolitical assumptions. These shifts have ignited calls for greater representation in institutions such as the UN Security Council, the World Bank, the WTO, and the IMF. The landscape of International Law is changing before our eyes.

In this multipolar world, the mechanisms for resolving disputes must evolve as well. While formal legal processes remain essential, the global climate increasingly favors informal negotiations, political compromise, and diplomacy that prioritizes understanding over rigidity. Multilateral treaties may no longer be the sole instruments of global governance; instead, we see a growing reliance on cultural intelligence, soft power, and the subtle art of dialogue.

It is true that both legal rules and cultural rules originate from the same human need: the need to coexist. Yet we must remember that cultural formations—family structures, religious ideologies, social dependencies, thought patterns, and learned attitudes—shape how societies perceive and respond to the rule of law. For law to fulfill its role in maintaining coexistence, legal authorities must understand the cultural significance of their actions. They must respect common cultural goals, acknowledge the power of informal social authority, and recognize that Cultural Diplomacy is not ornamental—it is essential. History repeatedly shows that the informal authority of society can be more powerful than formal law in shaping behavior. Thus, understanding culture is not optional; it is foundational to peace, stability, and human coexistence.

The cohabitation of International Law and international cultural interaction is not only possible—it is already present. When legal authorities tap into the immense power of Cultural Diplomacy, they do more than strengthen the rule of law; they create pathways for mutual understanding, for peace, and for sustainable development grounded in shared benefits. Cultural Diplomacy, when properly understood and applied, has the capacity to influence public sentiment, reshape belief systems, and connect people across borders in ways that formal agreements alone cannot achieve.

Cultural Diplomacy can facilitate worldwide intercultural discourse, global dialogue, justice, collaboration, human rights, peace, and harmony. These are not abstract ideals; they are the very objectives International Law seeks to protect. The convergence of these aims reveals a profound truth: law and culture are partners in the pursuit of a more just and peaceful world.

In this emerging multipolar order, lawmakers and international lawyers must cultivate new competencies. They must learn to lead difficult conversations, articulate their concerns with tact, and engage diplomatically without inflaming tensions. Cross-cultural literacy is no longer a peripheral skill—it is central to governing International Law and navigating international relations. The future will belong to those who can interpret not only statutes and treaties, but also societies, sentiments, and the subtle rhythms of human interaction.

Cohabitation: An Organic Human Need

The cohabitation of International Law and international cultural interaction is neither accidental nor peripheral; it is an organic convergence born from humanity's shared need to coexist. International Law, in its essence, seeks to regulate conduct among states and global actors, while culture shapes the values, behaviors, and expectations that guide societies. When these two forces meet, they do not collide—they inform one another. Legal norms gain depth when interpreted through cultural lenses, and cultural practices find structure when supported by legal frameworks. This interplay reveals that law cannot be fully understood without culture, just as culture cannot be fully protected without law. Their coexistence is therefore not merely possible but necessary for a world striving toward harmony.

As global interactions intensify, cultural dynamics increasingly influence how International Law is perceived, applied, and contested. Legal obligations may be universal in form, yet their reception varies across societies shaped by distinct histories, traditions, and belief systems. A treaty drafted in one cultural context may be interpreted differently in another, not out of defiance but out of deeply rooted cultural logic. This is why international cultural interaction becomes indispensable: it provides the interpretive bridge that allows legal norms to travel across borders without losing meaning. Through cultural exchange, dialogue, and diplomacy, states and communities gain the capacity to understand not only the letter of the law but the spirit in which it was crafted.

In practice, the cohabitation of law and culture becomes most visible in the informal spaces where diplomacy unfolds. While formal legal mechanisms remain essential for dispute resolution, the shifting global order increasingly favors negotiation, cultural intelligence, and soft power. Informal dialogues, cultural diplomacy initiatives, and cross-cultural engagements often succeed where rigid legalism falters. These interactions humanize the legal process, allowing states and actors to approach conflicts with empathy rather than antagonism. In a multipolar world, where power is dispersed and alliances are fluid, the ability to navigate cultural differences becomes as critical as the ability to interpret legal texts.

Ultimately, the partnership between International Law and international cultural interaction offers a pathway toward a more peaceful and equitable global society. When legal authorities recognize the power of culture, they unlock new avenues for cooperation, understanding, and conflict prevention. Cultural Diplomacy, in particular, becomes a catalyst—shaping public sentiment, influencing belief systems, and fostering networks of trust that transcend political boundaries. In this shared space, law gains legitimacy, culture gains protection, and humanity gains the possibility of coexistence grounded in mutual respect. The future of global governance will depend not on choosing between law or culture, but on embracing their cohabitation as the foundation for justice, stability, and harmony.

International Law: Where Need for Dialogue Is More Pronounced

Dialogue among those who interpret, enact, and enforce laws is indispensable because law does not operate in a vacuum. Every legal provision, every judicial decision, and every enforcement action is filtered through human understanding—shaped by cultural assumptions, historical memory, and societal expectations. When judges, lawmakers, and legal authorities engage in sustained dialogue, they create a shared interpretive space where the meaning of law becomes clearer, more coherent, and more responsive to the realities of society. Without such dialogue, law risks becoming fragmented, misunderstood, or misapplied, especially in a world where cultural diversity profoundly influences how justice is perceived and practiced.

In the international arena, this need for dialogue becomes even more pronounced. International Law is interpreted not by a single authority but by a constellation of actors—states, courts, international organizations, corporations, and civil society. Each brings its own cultural lens, legal tradition, and political interest. Dialogue becomes the mechanism through which these diverse perspectives negotiate meaning, reconcile differences, and build consensus. It is through conversation, consultation, and cultural exchange that international norms gain legitimacy and durability.

Without this communicative process, International Law would remain an abstract framework, disconnected from the lived experiences of the global community it seeks to govern.

Moreover, dialogue serves as a safeguard against the misuse or misinterpretation of legal authority. When those who enforce laws communicate openly with those who craft and interpret them, they create a feedback loop that strengthens accountability and transparency. Cultural Diplomacy plays a vital role here, offering tools to navigate sensitive conversations, bridge misunderstandings, and foster trust across borders. In a multipolar world marked by shifting alliances and rising tensions, the ability to engage in culturally informed dialogue becomes essential for preventing conflict and ensuring that legal decisions are grounded in mutual respect rather than unilateral assertion.

Ultimately, the indispensability of dialogue lies in its capacity to humanize the law. It transforms legal processes from rigid mechanisms into living systems capable of adapting to cultural change, social evolution, and global transformation. Through dialogue, legal actors learn to listen—to understand not only the text of the law but the cultural narratives that give it meaning. This shared understanding becomes the foundation for justice that is both principled and compassionate, for governance that is both effective and culturally attuned. In this sense, dialogue is not simply a procedural necessity; it is the lifeblood of a legal order that aspires to serve humanity with wisdom, dignity, and harmony.

Legal Processes: Understanding Over Rigidity:

In this multipolar world, the mechanisms for resolving disputes must evolve as well. While formal legal processes remain essential, the global climate increasingly favors informal negotiations, political compromise, and diplomacy that prioritizes understanding over rigidity. The rise of new economic powers, shifting alliances, and the reconfiguration of global influence have created a landscape where traditional legal instruments alone cannot address the complexity of contemporary disputes (Acharya, 2018). The world is no longer governed by a single hegemonic voice;

instead, it is shaped by a chorus of actors—states, corporations, civil society, and transnational networks—each with its own cultural logic and political priorities. In such an environment, flexibility, dialogue, and cultural intelligence become indispensable tools for maintaining stability (Slaughter, 2004).

Recent global crises illustrate this shift vividly. The ongoing tensions in the South China Sea demonstrate how formal legal rulings—such as the 2016 Permanent Court of Arbitration decision—may carry legal weight but lack enforceability without diplomatic engagement (Permanent Court of Arbitration, 2016). States involved continue to rely on back-channel negotiations, regional dialogues, and culturally informed diplomacy to prevent escalation. Similarly, the Russia-Ukraine conflict has exposed the limitations of formal international mechanisms when geopolitical interests collide. Sanctions, UN resolutions, and legal condemnations have symbolic and structural importance, yet the most meaningful progress toward humanitarian corridors, prisoner exchanges, and energy agreements has emerged through informal negotiations and mediated dialogue (United Nations, 2022). These examples underscore that law alone cannot resolve disputes in a world where power is dispersed and political realities are fluid.

The global political economy further reinforces the need for adaptive dispute-resolution mechanisms. Supply chain disruptions, energy dependencies, and the weaponization of economic interdependence have created new forms of conflict that transcend traditional legal categories (Farrell & Newman, 2019). The competition over critical minerals, the restructuring of global trade routes, and the rise of digital sovereignty disputes all require solutions that blend legal frameworks with diplomatic pragmatism. For instance, the ongoing debates around data governance and cross-border digital regulation cannot be settled solely through treaties; they demand continuous dialogue among states, tech corporations, and international bodies (UNCTAD, 2021). These issues reveal that the future of dispute resolution lies in hybrid approaches—where law provides structure, but diplomacy provides movement.

Moreover, the growing influence of regional organizations and non-state actors has diversified the channels through which disputes are addressed. The African Union, ASEAN, the Gulf Cooperation Council, and the South American Community of Nations increasingly rely on culturally grounded negotiation practices that emphasize consensus, relational trust, and incremental progress (Katzenstein, 1996). These approaches often succeed where rigid legalism fails because they acknowledge the cultural dimensions of conflict. In many regions, informal authority—elders, religious leaders, community networks—still plays a decisive role in shaping outcomes. International Law must therefore coexist with these cultural mechanisms, recognizing that legitimacy is often earned through cultural resonance rather than legal formality.

Ultimately, the evolution of dispute-resolution mechanisms reflects a deeper truth: peace is sustained not by rules alone, but by relationships. A multipolar world requires legal actors who can navigate cultural differences, interpret political signals, and engage in dialogue that humanizes the parties involved. Diplomacy that prioritizes understanding over rigidity does not weaken the law; it strengthens it by ensuring that legal norms remain relevant, adaptable, and grounded in the lived realities of global society (Bercovitch & Jackson, 2009). As international challenges grow more interconnected—from climate migration to cyber conflict—the ability to blend legal reasoning with cultural diplomacy will determine whether the international community can manage disputes peacefully or succumb to fragmentation. The future of global governance depends on this delicate, indispensable balance.

Cultural Diplomacy: A Pilar of Treaty Interpretation and Customary Law

Cultural Diplomacy can facilitate worldwide intercultural discourse, global dialogue, justice, collaboration, human rights, peace, and harmony. These aspirations are not merely moral ideals; they mirror the foundational objectives embedded in the International Law of Treaties. Every treaty is born from negotiation, and negotiation itself is a cultural act—shaped by language, symbolism, historical memory, and the interpersonal dynamics of the parties involved. The

Vienna Convention on the Law of Treaties emphasizes good faith, mutual consent, and the shared intention of states, yet these principles cannot be realized without cultural understanding. Cultural Diplomacy strengthens the interpretive environment in which treaties are drafted and applied, ensuring that obligations are understood not only legally but contextually, reducing the risk of misinterpretation and fostering trust among states.

Customary International Law is equally intertwined with cultural interaction. Custom emerges from consistent state practice and the belief that such practice is legally required, but these behaviors are deeply influenced by cultural norms, regional traditions, and collective expectations. When states engage in cultural exchange—through dialogue, education, artistic collaboration, or diplomatic outreach—they shape the very social fabric from which customary norms evolve. Cultural Diplomacy accelerates the formation of shared understandings about what constitutes lawful, ethical, or acceptable conduct. In areas such as diplomatic immunity, humanitarian principles, or the treatment of foreign nationals, customary norms have historically crystallized through repeated intercultural encounters long before they were codified in treaties.

The convergence of Cultural Diplomacy with treaty law and customary law reveals a profound truth: law and culture are partners in the pursuit of a more just and peaceful world. Treaties provide structure, custom provides continuity, and culture provides meaning. Without cultural bridges, legal commitments risk becoming rigid texts detached from lived realities. With Cultural Diplomacy, however, International Law becomes a living framework—capable of adapting to diverse societies, mediating differences, and fostering cooperation grounded in mutual respect. In this partnership, culture animates the law, and the law safeguards the values culture seeks to uphold. Together, they create the conditions for global harmony, human dignity, and sustainable peace.

Final Thoughts:

I am convinced that the harmony we seek in global governance will not be achieved through law alone, nor through culture alone, but through their thoughtful and intentional cohabitation. International Law provides the structure—the treaties, the norms, the obligations that bind states to predictable conduct—yet culture provides the meaning that allows these commitments to resonate across societies. Without cultural understanding, even the most carefully drafted treaty risks becoming an empty vessel, interpreted rigidly or resisted silently. Without legal frameworks, cultural aspirations for peace and justice lack the mechanisms to be realized. It is in the meeting of these two forces that humanity finds its most promising path toward coexistence.

This cohabitation becomes especially vital in a multipolar world where power is dispersed, identities are plural, and global challenges transcend borders. Customary norms evolve through shared practice, and treaties endure through mutual respect—both of which depend on dialogue, empathy, and cultural literacy. Cultural Diplomacy enriches this process by humanizing international engagement, enabling states to see beyond their own legal traditions and appreciate the values that shape others' interpretations of justice. When legal actors understand the cultural roots of behavior, and when cultural actors appreciate the stabilizing role of law, disputes can be approached not as zero-sum contests but as opportunities for collaborative problem-solving. This is how International Law becomes not merely enforceable, but meaningful.

In closing, the future of global governance rests on our willingness to embrace this duality. Law gives us the tools to articulate rights and responsibilities; culture gives us the wisdom to apply them with compassion. Together, they form a framework capable of sustaining peace, nurturing justice, and honoring human dignity. If we aspire to a world where humanity coexists with respect—where treaties are upheld not out of fear but out of shared purpose, and where customary norms reflect our highest collective values—then we must commit to this partnership. The harmony we seek is not a distant ideal; it is a deliberate choice, forged at the intersection of legal order and cultural understanding, and carried forward by those who believe that a more peaceful world is both possible and worth pursuing.

The references for this briefing are provided on page 298.

Briefing 7.

UNESCO CONVENTIONS AND STATE BEHAVIOR

In Brief:

UNESCO conventions stand as some of the most subtle yet powerful instruments in the architecture of international cooperation. They do not coerce states; rather, they cultivate them. Their influence lies not in force, but in the moral authority and shared vision they inspire among nations. In this sense, UNESCO's legal instruments operate as a quiet compass, guiding states toward higher standards of cultural responsibility, educational advancement, and ethical stewardship.

At their core, these conventions articulate a collective promise: that humanity's cultural and intellectual heritage is not the property of one nation, but the shared inheritance of all. When states ratify these instruments, they are not merely accepting legal obligations — they are aligning themselves with a global ethic. They commit to safeguarding heritage, promoting cultural diversity, advancing education, and fostering scientific cooperation. And in doing so, they signal to the world the kind of leadership they aspire to embody.

UNESCO conventions, while formally treaty instruments, frequently function as incubators of customary norms. Through repeated state practice—legislative enactments, administrative measures, judicial citations—and the concomitant expression of *opinio juris (short for opinio juris sive necessitates / an opinion of law or necessity)*, the principles enshrined in these instruments migrate from negotiated text into the fabric of general international law. This process is neither automatic nor uniform; it depends on the visibility of the practice, the clarity of the normative statement, and the extent to which states treat the obligation as legally binding rather than merely aspirational.

The conventions also perform an interpretive work that shapes how customary rules are understood and applied. Domestic courts and international tribunals often look to treaty language and the interpretive materials produced under UNESCO's aegis to resolve ambiguities in customary norms, thereby reinforcing a coherent normative architecture. In this way, treaty-based standards and customary law engage in a reciprocal dialogue: conventions crystallize emerging norms, and customary practice, once consolidated, informs the evolution and application of treaty obligations.

For scholars and practitioners concerned with the legitimacy and efficacy of international law, the lesson is clear: attention must be paid not only to the text of conventions but to the ecosystem of implementation that gives them life. Monitoring state practice, documenting opinio juris, and scrutinizing the domestic uptake of UNESCO principles are essential tasks if we are to understand how soft commitments harden into binding expectations. Only by tracing that trajectory can we appreciate the conventions' true legal force and their capacity to reconfigure state behaviour in service of a shared cultural and intellectual patrimony.

UNESCO's conventions shape state behavior in three profound ways:

1. Establishing Normative Expectations:

UNESCO's conventions function as a kind of ethical metronome: they set the tempo at which states are expected to move, even when no formal sanction compels them. Once a norm is articulated in a UNESCO instrument, it enters the bloodstream of international discourse. Governments begin to reference it in policy statements, courts cite it as persuasive authority, and civil society invokes it as a benchmark for evaluating state performance. Over time, this creates a gravitational pull — a sense that deviation is not merely a legal omission but a reputational lapse.

These expectations also shape domestic political incentives. Ministers, cultural agencies, and educational authorities know that alignment with UNESCO standards signals competence and modernity. As a result, states internalize these norms not only to avoid criticism but to demonstrate that they are attuned to global priorities. The conventions thus operate as a subtle but persistent reminder that sovereignty today is exercised in dialogue with shared human values, not in isolation from them.

A clear example is the **1972 World Heritage Convention**, which has shaped how states understand their obligations toward cultural and natural heritage. Even without coercive enforcement, the Convention has created a global expectation that states must inventory, protect, and manage sites of "Outstanding Universal Value." When the Great Barrier Reef was considered for inscription on the List of World Heritage in Danger, Australia undertook significant policy reforms — including new water-quality targets and reef-management plans — to avoid reputational damage and demonstrate compliance with UNESCO's standards (UNESCO, 2021). This illustrates how the Convention's norms exert pressure long before any formal sanction is applied.

Similarly, the **2003 Convention for the Safeguarding of Intangible Cultural Heritage** has normalized the idea that living traditions — from craftsmanship to oral traditions — require state support. Countries such as Japan, Morocco, and Peru have expanded national safeguarding programs not because UNESCO compels them, but because the Convention has set a global benchmark for what responsible cultural governance looks like (UNESCO, 2020).

2. Fostering Collaborative Accountability:

The collaborative architecture surrounding UNESCO conventions transforms compliance from a solitary act into a collective enterprise. Reporting cycles, peer review processes, and technical exchanges create a rhythm of mutual observation. States see not only how they measure up but how others innovate, adapt, and overcome similar challenges. This comparative visibility generates a constructive pressure: no state wishes to be the one that lags behind when progress is publicly charted.

Moreover, the collaborative dimension builds capacity rather than merely evaluating performance. Through expert missions, training programs, and shared methodologies, states learn from one another and refine their own systems. Accountability becomes less about surveillance and more about co-development. In this way, UNESCO's conventions cultivate a community of practice — one in which states advance together, drawing strength from the collective rather than competing in isolation.

The example of the above mechanism is, UNESCO's **Periodic Reporting** under the World Heritage Convention is a prime example of collaborative accountability. States submit detailed reports on the condition of their sites, which are then reviewed regionally and internationally. This process allows states to compare their progress, identify shared challenges, and adopt best practices. For instance, African and Arab States have used the reporting cycle to coordinate training programs on risk preparedness and site management, improving outcomes across multiple countries (UNESCO, 2019).

Another example is the **Global Education Monitoring (GEM) Report**, which supports the implementation of the Education 2030 Framework for Action. Although not a convention, it operates in tandem with UNESCO's normative instruments. Countries voluntarily share data on access, equity, and learning outcomes, creating a transparent environment where progress is visible and peer comparison encourages improvement. The collaborative nature of the reporting process has helped countries like Vietnam and

Rwanda refine their national education strategies based on shared evidence (UNESCO, 2022).

3. Elevating Soft Power Incentives:

UNESCO's conventions also operate in the realm of symbolic capital. States that visibly champion cultural protection, educational equity, or scientific cooperation accrue a form of soft power that cannot be purchased or coerced. They position themselves as guardians of humanity's shared inheritance, and this moral posture enhances their diplomatic credibility. In multilateral settings, such reputational assets often translate into influence, trust, and leadership opportunities.

This soft power dynamic also resonates domestically. Governments that align with UNESCO principles can present themselves to their citizens as forward-looking, culturally responsible, and globally engaged. The conventions thus become instruments of national branding — a way for states to narrate who they are and what they stand for. In a world where legitimacy increasingly depends on values as much as on power, this reputational dimension is not peripheral; it is central to how states navigate the international stage.

For example, soft power is most visible in the global prestige associated with **World Heritage inscription**. Countries actively campaign for inscription because it signals cultural sophistication, responsible stewardship, and international credibility. Italy and France, for example, frequently highlight their World Heritage sites in diplomatic and cultural outreach, using UNESCO recognition to reinforce their identity as custodians of global heritage (UNESCO, 2023). The incentive is reputational, not legal — yet it powerfully shapes state behavior.

Similarly, states leverage UNESCO's **Creative Cities Network** to enhance their global standing in fields such as gastronomy, literature, and design. Cities like Seoul (Design), Bologna (Music), and Oaxaca (Gastronomy) use their UNESCO designation to attract investment, tourism, and cultural partnerships. These recognitions operate as soft-power assets, demonstrating that the state or city is aligned with UNESCO's values of creativity, sustainability, and cultural diversity (UNESCO, 2023).

Culture as a Compass: How UNESCO Quietly Turns Norms into Customary Law

When I examine UNESCO's conventions through the lens of my own work on customary law, I am reminded that law does not emerge from coercion; it emerges from culture. It is culture that gives law its texture, its resonance, and ultimately its legitimacy. Thus, when UNESCO articulates normative expectations, I see more than treaty language — I see the slow, deliberate shaping of a shared moral horizon. These conventions cultivate a sense of what is appropriate, what is responsible, and what is worthy of the international community's respect. States respond to these expectations not because they fear sanction, but because they recognize the cultural weight behind them. In this way, UNESCO's instruments operate much like customary norms themselves: they take root through repetition, affirmation, and the quiet but persistent force of collective belief.

In the collaborative mechanisms that UNESCO fosters, I see another familiar dynamic. Customary law grows through interaction — through states observing one another, learning from one another, and adjusting their conduct in a shared normative space. UNESCO's reporting cycles, peer reviews, and cooperative frameworks embody this very process. They transform compliance into a cultural practice, a ritual of transparency and mutual refinement. When states participate in these mechanisms, they are not merely fulfilling procedural requirements; they are engaging in the very dialogue through which norms mature. This is accountability not as surveillance, but as solidarity — a recognition that the stewardship of culture, education, and heritage is a collective responsibility.

And when I consider the soft-power incentives embedded in UNESCO's work, I am reminded that culture has always been a form of strategic capital. Nations that champion UNESCO's principles do more than comply with international expectations; they position themselves as custodians of shared human values. This is a form of leadership that does not rely on force or dominance, but on example. It is the kind of leadership that elevates a state's standing because it demonstrates cultural maturity, ethical responsibility, and a willingness to contribute to the global commons. In my view, this is where culture and law converge most powerfully: when the symbolic becomes structural, when the aspirational becomes habitual, and when the ethical becomes customary.

In all of this, I see UNESCO's conventions not as external impositions, but as cultural instruments that help shape the moral architecture of the international system. They remind us that law is, at its core, a cultural achievement — a reflection of who we are, what we value, and what we aspire to protect. And in that sense, UNESCO's work is deeply aligned with the very foundations of customary law: it nurtures the shared understandings from which enduring norms are born.

In essence, UNESCO conventions do not dictate; they inspire. They do not impose; they invite. Their true strength lies in their ability to shape the conscience of nations — to encourage states to act not only in accordance with law, but in harmony with the values that bind humanity together. This is the kind of influence that endures, because it transforms behavior from within.

And when we speak of influence that transforms from within, we are also speaking of the slow, deliberate work of cultivating shared imaginaries. UNESCO's conventions help states imagine themselves not merely as sovereign actors pursuing national interests, but as participants in a broader human project. This shift in self-perception is subtle yet profound. It reframes compliance not as obligation but as contribution, and it encourages nations to see cultural stewardship as a marker of legitimacy rather than a diplomatic accessory. In this way, UNESCO nurtures the psychological conditions under which global norms can take root.

This internalization of values is especially important in a world where geopolitical tensions often overshadow cooperative instincts. When states adopt UNESCO's frameworks, they are not simply aligning with international standards; they are affirming that culture, heritage, and knowledge are global goods that transcend political cycles. Such commitments create pockets of stability in an otherwise volatile system. They remind us that even in moments of discord, there remain shared foundations upon which dialogue and trust can be rebuilt.

Moreover, the conventions offer a blueprint for how states can operationalize cultural responsibility. They provide mechanisms for safeguarding heritage, promoting education, and fostering intercultural understanding — not as abstract ideals, but as actionable policies. These instruments help governments translate values into practice, enabling them to build institutions that reflect both national identity and global solidarity. In doing so, UNESCO's work becomes a bridge between aspiration and implementation, between the symbolic and the structural.

Ultimately, what UNESCO offers is not merely a set of legal tools, but a vision of international life grounded in reciprocity and respect. Its conventions remind us that global governance is most effective when it is anchored in shared meaning rather than coercive power. They invite states to participate in a collective narrative about who we are and who we might become. And in accepting that invitation, nations contribute to a more coherent, humane, and culturally attuned international order — one in which law and culture evolve together, shaping a future worthy of our highest ideals.

In Closing:

In drawing these threads together, I return to a conviction that has guided much of my work: law endures only when it is nourished by culture. UNESCO's conventions, in all their quiet influence, remind us that the international system is not held together by force, but by shared understandings — by the norms we internalize, the responsibilities we accept, and the values we choose to elevate. Their capacity to set expectations, to cultivate collaborative accountability, and to inspire soft-power leadership demonstrates that culture remains the most durable architect of legal order.

What we witness in UNESCO's instruments is not merely the administration of treaties, but the slow formation of customary pathways — the emergence of habits, practices, and beliefs that shape how states see themselves and how they wish to be seen. This is the subtle alchemy through which culture becomes norm, and norm becomes law. It is also the space where states rediscover their agency: not as subjects of obligation, but as co-authors of a shared moral horizon. If there is a lesson to carry forward, it is that the future of international law will depend less on the rigidity of its rules and more on the vitality of its cultural foundations.

Where culture is honored, law finds legitimacy. Where dialogue is sustained, norms find coherence. And where states lead through example rather than assertion, the international community finds its compass.

In this sense, UNESCO's conventions do more than guide state behavior — they remind us of what is possible when culture is treated not as ornament, but as origin. They call us back to the simple but profound truth that the most enduring legal commitments are those rooted in the shared inheritance of humanity. And it is there, in that common ground, that customary law continues to live, evolve, and quietly shape the world we are building together.

References:

UNESCO. (2019). *World Heritage Convention: Periodic Reporting – Regional Overviews*. UNESCO World Heritage Centre.

UNESCO. (2020). *Convention for the Safeguarding of the Intangible Cultural Heritage: Implementation Reports*. UNESCO.

UNESCO. (2021). *State of Conservation Report: Great Barrier Reef (Australia)*. UNESCO World Heritage Centre.

UNESCO. (2022). *Global Education Monitoring Report 2022*. UNESCO.

UNESCO. (2023). *UNESCO World Heritage List & Creative Cities Network – Annual Highlights*. UNESCO.

"Throughout the history of mankind, every leader who preached peace, was accompanied by armed people."

Mosi Dorbayani

Briefing 8.
INTERNATIONAL LAW AND THE SOVEREIGNTY OF SMALL AND VULNERABLE STATES

In Brief:

Sovereignty has long been regarded as the cornerstone of the international legal order, but in today's rapidly shifting geopolitical landscape, it carries an even deeper resonance. Beyond its legal definition as supreme authority within a territory, sovereignty functions as a sacred space—a protected realm in which a nation's identity, values, and collective aspirations are cultivated. It is within this space that societies articulate who they are, how they wish to be governed, and what vision they hold for their future. As global interdependence intensifies, the sanctity of this space becomes both more precious and more contested, demanding renewed attention to its meaning and implications.

For many states—particularly those with fragile histories, diverse populations, or emerging political institutions—sovereignty is not merely a juridical status but a vessel of self-determination. It embodies the right of a people to define their cultural narrative, preserve their heritage, and pursue development according to their own priorities.

When external pressures—whether geopolitical, economic, or ideological—encroach upon this domain, they threaten more than administrative autonomy; they risk eroding the very foundations of national identity. Thus, safeguarding sovereignty becomes synonymous with safeguarding the dignity and continuity of a nation's cultural and political life.

Yet the contemporary world presents a paradox. Global challenges such as climate change, digital governance, migration, and transnational conflict require unprecedented cooperation, often blurring traditional boundaries of authority. In this environment, sovereignty must be reimagined not as isolation, but as a dynamic equilibrium between internal self-definition and external engagement. Treating sovereignty as a sacred space does not imply rigidity; rather, it underscores the need for international frameworks that respect national identities while enabling collective action. This balance—between autonomy and interdependence—will shape the future of global governance and determine whether nations can thrive without sacrificing the essence of who they are.

With all the above in mind, one may ask: then why international laws are not supporting Ukraine?

This is a powerful and understandable question, and it comes up often when people look at the gap between what international law promises and what actually happens on the ground. The short answer is this: international law does support Ukraine—but international law has no automatic enforcement mechanism, and great-power politics often overwhelms legal norms. Let me unpack this in a clear, structured way.

Why It Feels Like International Law Is Not Supporting Ukraine:

1. International law is clear: Russia's invasion is illegal—but law alone cannot stop force

   Under the UN Charter, the use of force against another state is prohibited except in self-defense or with UN Security Council authorization. Russia's invasion violates these principles.

   So legally, Ukraine is supported.

The problem is that international law does not have its own police force. It relies on states to enforce it, and when a powerful state violates the law, the system struggles to respond effectively.

This is the core tension:

Law defines what should happen; power determines what does happen.

2. The UN Security Council is paralyzed by the veto system

The Security Council is supposed to maintain international peace and security. But one of its permanent members— Russia—is the aggressor. Because Russia holds veto power, it can block any binding resolution against itself. This is not a failure of law; it is a failure of institutional design:

The UN was built after World War II to prevent conflict between great powers, not to restrain them.

So the system works well when small or medium states break the rules, but it breaks down when a major power does.

3. International law works through slow, cumulative mechanisms—not instant solutions

Ukraine has received significant legal support:

- ✓ Cases at the International Court of Justice
- ✓ Investigations by the International Criminal Court
- ✓ Global sanctions regimes
- ✓ Recognition of territorial integrity by most states
- ✓ UN General Assembly resolutions condemning the invasion

These actions matter, but they are long-term tools, not immediate shields.

International law is like a glacier: slow, heavy, and powerful over time—but not fast enough to stop tanks in real time.

So why does it look like "international law is not supporting Ukraine"?

Because international law is not designed to overpower military force directly.

- ➤ It is designed to:
- ➤ Delegitimize aggression;

- ➤ Mobilize global pressure;
- ➤ Isolate violators;
- ➤ Create long-term accountability; and,
- ➤ Shape post-conflict outcomes.

But it cannot physically prevent a powerful state from using force.

This is the uncomfortable truth:

International law is strongest when states choose to respect it—and weakest when great powers choose to ignore it.

International Law and Sovereignty of Greenland:

I am often asked by my students: *"If Sovereignty Is Sacred, Why Doesn't International Law Do More for Greenland?"*

Greenland is not facing an invasion like Ukraine, but it is at the center of a quiet geopolitical contest. The question often arises because Greenland's vast territory, strategic Arctic location, and natural resources make it highly attractive to major powers. Yet Greenland's sovereignty situation is complex: it is not an independent state, but an autonomous territory within the Kingdom of Denmark. That creates a different legal landscape—and explains why international law operates differently there.

Here is a clear unpacking of the issue:

1. Greenland is not a fully sovereign state—so international law treats it differently. Unlike Ukraine, Greenland does not have full international legal personality. It has:
- Extensive self-rule;
- Control over internal governance; and,
- The right to pursue independence if it chooses.

But Denmark retains responsibility for:

- ✓ Foreign affairs;
- ✓ Defense; and,
- ✓ Certain constitutional matters.

Because of this structure, international law does not treat Greenland as a separate state whose sovereignty can be violated. Any external pressure—economic, strategic, or political—is technically directed at Denmark, not Greenland itself.

This means the legal tools available to Ukraine simply do not apply in the same way to Greenland.

2. The "threat" to Greenland is not military invasion but strategic influence.

Greenland's situation is shaped by:

- US military presence in the Arctic;
- China's interest in mining and infrastructure;
- Russia's Arctic militarization; and,
- Climate-driven competition for shipping routes and resources.

These pressures are subtle, economic, and strategic, not overt violations of territorial integrity.

International law is much better at addressing:

✓ Armed aggression.
✓ Occupation.
✓ Annexation.

It is far weaker at regulating:

- ➤ Foreign investment.
- ➤ Influence campaigns.
- ➤ Economic dependency.
- ➤ Strategic competition.

So even when great powers compete for influence in Greenland, *it does not trigger the same legal protections that Ukraine can invoke.*

3. Greenland's sovereignty is protected primarily through political choices, not legal enforcement

Because Greenland is part of Denmark, its protection comes from:

- ✓ Denmark's diplomatic alliances;
- ✓ NATO membership;
- ✓ EU partnerships (even though Greenland itself is not in the EU); and,
- ✓ Denmark's constitutional guarantees of Greenlandic self-rule.

In other words, Greenland's sovereignty is shielded by political structures, not by international legal enforcement mechanisms.

International law supports:

- ✓ The right to self-determination.
- ✓ The right to decolonization.
- ✓ The right to internal autonomy.

But it does not intervene unless:

- ➤ A state is attacked.
- ➤ A population is denied its right to choose its political future.
- ➤ Human rights are violated.

None of these thresholds have been crossed in Greenland.

So why does it feel like international law isn't "doing more" for Greenland?

Because Greenland's challenges are not legal violations— *they are geopolitical realities.*

International law is designed to respond to breaches of sovereignty, not to:

- Prevent great-power interest.
- Regulate foreign investment.
- Stop strategic competition.
- Manage Arctic militarization.

Greenland's situation is therefore shaped more by:

- ➤ Diplomacy;
- ➤ Alliances;
- ➤ Internal political decisions; and,
- ➤ Economic strategy than by legal enforcement.

Moving on, let us next examine how smalls states can safeguard themselves.

How Small States Can Safeguard Sovereignty Amid Great-Power Rivalry:

Small states often find themselves navigating a geopolitical landscape shaped by actors far larger and more powerful than themselves. Yet history shows that small states are not merely passive objects of great-power competition; they can be remarkably resilient when they adopt strategies that reinforce sovereignty as both a legal shield and a political asset. In an era of renewed rivalry among major powers, safeguarding sovereignty requires a combination of diplomatic agility, institutional strength, and strategic diversification.

First, small states protect their sovereignty by anchoring themselves in international law and multilateral institutions. Bodies such as the United Nations, regional organizations, and international courts provide platforms where the legal equality of states is recognized and defended. For small states, these institutions act as force multipliers: they amplify their voice, constrain unilateral pressure from larger powers, and create predictable frameworks for dispute resolution. By actively participating in treaty regimes, arbitration mechanisms, and collective security arrangements, small states reinforce the principle that sovereignty is not negotiable, even when power is unevenly distributed.

Second, sovereignty is strengthened when small states pursue strategic diversification—economically, diplomatically, and militarily. Overreliance on a single great power exposes a state to coercion; diversification reduces vulnerability. This can include expanding trade partnerships, cultivating multiple security relationships, and engaging in regional alliances that provide collective leverage. Some small states also adopt "smart neutrality," maintaining balanced relations with competing powers while positioning themselves as hubs for finance, diplomacy, or innovation. By doing so, they transform their small size into a form of strategic flexibility rather than weakness.

Finally, the most enduring safeguard of sovereignty lies in domestic resilience. Strong institutions, transparent governance, social cohesion, and economic stability make a state far harder to manipulate from the outside. When citizens trust their institutions and feel represented by them, external actors find fewer entry points for influence. Investing in education, cybersecurity, cultural preservation, and sustainable development strengthens the internal foundations of sovereignty. In this sense, sovereignty is not only a legal status but a lived reality—rooted in the capacity of a society to govern itself confidently and coherently.

The Future of Sovereignty in Digital and Cyber Domains:

The digital realm has become a new frontier in which the meaning of sovereignty is being renegotiated. Traditional sovereignty is grounded in territory, borders, and jurisdiction, yet cyberspace is inherently borderless, fast-moving, and shaped by actors who often operate beyond the reach of national legal systems. As states increasingly rely on digital infrastructure for governance, security, and economic life, the protection of this virtual domain becomes inseparable from the protection of sovereignty itself. The future of sovereignty will depend on how effectively states can assert authority over digital spaces without undermining the openness and interoperability that make the internet a global common.

One of the most significant transformations lies in the shift from territorial sovereignty to digital sovereignty—the ability of a state to control data flows, regulate digital platforms, and secure its cyber infrastructure. Small and large states alike are developing legal frameworks to govern data localization, cybersecurity standards, and the responsibilities of private tech giants whose platforms now function as quasi-public spaces. Yet this evolution raises complex questions: How far can a state go in regulating digital activity without fragmenting the global internet? How can international law reconcile the tension between national control and the inherently transnational nature of cyber threats? The answers will shape not only the future of digital governance but also the balance of power between states and corporations.

At the same time, sovereignty in the cyber domain will increasingly depend on resilience rather than control. Cyberattacks, disinformation campaigns, and digital espionage have become tools of geopolitical competition, often targeting the social fabric and political processes of states. Protecting sovereignty in this environment requires more than firewalls; it demands robust institutions, digital literacy, and societal cohesion. States that can safeguard their information ecosystems, maintain trust in public institutions, and ensure the integrity of their digital infrastructure will be better positioned to defend their autonomy. In this sense, the future of sovereignty is not only about asserting authority over cyberspace but about cultivating the internal strength to withstand the vulnerabilities that come with digital interdependence.

Here is a unified, fluent four-paragraph In Closing that weaves together both Part I and Part II into a single, coherent ending. It preserves the conceptual depth, avoids repetition, and maintains the reflective, scholarly tone of your full briefing.

In Closing:

Sovereignty remains one of the most profound organizing principles of the international order because it protects the inner life of a nation—its memory, its aspirations, and its right to define its own path. When that protected space is violated, the injury is not only territorial but existential. Ukraine's experience makes this painfully clear: the breach of sovereignty is also a breach of identity, dignity, and the collective narrative a people have built over generations. Yet the Ukrainian case also exposes the structural fragility of the global system. International law can articulate norms, condemn violations, and mobilize accountability, but it cannot compel powerful states to act against their interests. What emerges is a system that affirms Ukraine's rights in principle while lacking the mechanisms to enforce them in practice—a gap that is both morally troubling and strategically consequential.

Greenland's situation reveals a different facet of this tension. Here, sovereignty is not threatened by invasion but by the quiet gravitational pull of great-power interest. Its autonomy exists within a constitutional framework that places foreign affairs and defense under Denmark's authority, creating a legal landscape where international law does not treat Greenland as a fully sovereign actor. The pressures it faces—economic influence, strategic competition, and Arctic militarization—fall outside the categories international law was designed to regulate. As a result, Greenland's sovereignty is shaped less by legal enforcement and more by political architecture, demonstrating that vulnerability can arise even when no rule has been broken.

For small states, these realities underscore the need to cultivate sovereignty as both a legal shield and a strategic practice. Their resilience lies in anchoring themselves in multilateral norms while diversifying their economic, diplomatic, and security relationships. When small states strengthen their institutions, broaden their partnerships, and invest in societal cohesion, they transform sovereignty from a fragile status into a durable capability. This is not a defensive posture but a proactive one—an approach that treats sovereignty as something continuously reinforced through choices, alliances, and internal strength. In doing so, small states demonstrate that agency is not determined by size but by strategy.

As the world moves deeper into the digital age, the meaning of sovereignty will continue to evolve. The challenges emerging in cyberspace—data governance, digital infrastructure, information integrity—are not peripheral to statehood; they are becoming central to it. The states that thrive will be those that understand sovereignty not as a static inheritance but as a dynamic responsibility exercised across both physical and virtual domains. Whether in the

Arctic, in small-state diplomacy, or in the cyber realm, the future of sovereignty will depend on the capacity of nations to protect their identity, assert their agency, and adapt to a world where power is increasingly exercised through influence rather than invasion.

We need to remember that, *the sovereignty of nations is not a privilege granted by the powerful; it is a natural extension of a people's identity, culture, and historical journey.*

DIPLOMACY WITHOUT A PULSE:
A MANIFESTO FOR RE-HUMANIZING STATECRAFT

In Brief:

Diplomacy, in its classical form, was never merely the art of negotiation. It was the art of being human in the presence of difference. It was the ability to listen beyond words, to see beyond borders, and to speak beyond interests. Yet today, as the world accelerates toward hyper-modernity, diplomacy has become increasingly transactional—reduced to statements, summits, and sterile protocols. What is missing is not intelligence, nor strategy, nor technology. What is missing is **soul**.

The Erosion of Cultural Consciousness:

Modern diplomacy often treats culture as an accessory—something to be displayed at ceremonies or invoked in speeches. But culture is not decoration; it is the very fabric of human identity. Without cultural consciousness, diplomacy becomes a negotiation between abstractions rather than between people. We have forgotten that a nation is not a flag or a GDP figure. A nation is its poets, its elders, its rituals, its collective memory. When diplomats fail to engage with these deeper layers, they negotiate only with the surface of a society, never its heart. Cultural diplomacy is not a soft alternative to "real" diplomacy; it is the foundation upon which all sustainable agreements rest.

When culture is sidelined, diplomacy loses its moral compass. A diplomat who does not understand the cultural psyche of a people cannot speak to their aspirations, their fears, or their sense of dignity. Such diplomacy becomes transactional—void of empathy, void of resonance, void of the human truth that binds societies together. Culture is the silent negotiator in every room, the unspoken context that shapes meaning long before words are exchanged. To ignore it is to negotiate blindfolded.

And so, the erosion of cultural consciousness is not merely an academic concern; it is a strategic vulnerability. When nations forget the stories that shaped them, they become susceptible to narratives imposed from outside. When leaders dismiss the wisdom of their own traditions, they lose the ability to inspire their people toward shared purpose. Cultural diplomacy, therefore, is not an embellishment—it is a safeguard. It is the discipline that reminds us that peace is not engineered; it is cultivated. It grows from mutual recognition, from the humility to listen, and from the courage to honor the heritage that makes each nation distinct yet capable of harmony.

A Case Study in Cultural Diplomacy: Japan–South Korea Cultural Exchange (1998–2004)

One of the clearest contemporary examples—frequently examined in the literature on cultural diplomacy—is the reconciliation process between Japan and South Korea in the late 1990s and early 2000s, particularly following Japan's decision to lift long-standing restrictions on Korean cultural imports (Lee, 2012; Yoon, 2014). This period is compelling because it demonstrates how cultural understanding advanced where formal political negotiations had repeatedly stalled.

For decades, the bilateral relationship was marked by historical grievances, political mistrust, and recurring diplomatic impasses. Traditional diplomacy—centered on official statements, treaties, and high-level visits—made only incremental progress. A turning point emerged in 1998, when Japanese Prime Minister Keizo Obuchi and South Korean President Kim Dae-jung established a new partnership emphasizing mutual cultural appreciation (Obuchi & Kim, 1998). Japan subsequently lifted restrictions on Korean films, music, and television, while South Korea opened its cultural market to Japanese media. Joint cultural festivals, youth exchanges, and academic collaborations expanded rapidly during this period (Kim, 2005).

Why Cultural Diplomacy Worked:

Culture softened the political climate. Korean dramas, Japanese anime, literature, cuisine, and popular music created emotional familiarity between the two societies. Citizens increasingly viewed one another not as historical adversaries but as cultural neighbors (Iwabuchi, 2015). This shift in public sentiment preceded political agreement, giving leaders greater room to negotiate without domestic backlash. Shared cultural experiences also built trust: when millions of people consume each other's art, humor, and stories, they begin to understand the emotional landscape of the other nation—something no treaty can replicate.

Outcomes of the Cultural Thaw:

This cultural opening laid the groundwork for expanded trade agreements, the joint hosting of the 2002 FIFA World Cup, more stable diplomatic dialogue, and a generation of youth in both countries who grew up with fewer prejudices (Cho, 2016). Although political tensions continue to surface today, the cultural bridge constructed during this period remains resilient and continues to influence diplomatic engagement.

Why This Example Matters:

The Japan–Korea case illustrates a broader truth: cultural understanding can succeed where political negotiation alone cannot. When nations connect through culture— through music, film, language, food, and shared stories— they create a foundation of empathy that makes political cooperation not only possible but sustainable.

The Decline of Empathic Leadership in Diplomacy:

Diplomacy today suffers from a deficit of empathy. We have mastered the language of policy but lost the language of humanity. Empathy is not weakness; it is strategic wisdom. It allows nations to anticipate conflict before it erupts, to understand grievances before they calcify, and to build trust before it becomes a rare commodity. Empathic leadership does not mean agreeing with the other side. It means recognizing their dignity, their fears, their aspirations. It means remembering that behind every political stance stands a human story.

Empathy is the discipline of listening beyond the spoken word—of discerning the tremor beneath a demand, the sorrow beneath a grievance, the hope beneath a proposal. When leaders approach the negotiation table with emotional intelligence, they do not dilute their national interests; they elevate them. They transform diplomacy from a contest of wills into a dialogue of futures. Empathic leadership is the art of seeing the human being before the geopolitical actor, and in doing so, discovering solutions that are both principled and enduring.

And so, the decline of empathy in diplomacy is not merely a moral failing; it is a strategic hazard. A world led by technocrats who cannot feel will inevitably drift toward policies that cannot heal. Without empathy, agreements become brittle, alliances become transactional, and peace becomes temporary. But when empathy is restored to leadership, diplomacy regains its most powerful instrument: the ability to transform adversaries into partners, and uncertainty into possibility. Empathy is not an accessory to statecraft—it is the quiet force that makes statecraft humane, credible, and ultimately sustainable as this creates a healthy rhythm for a peaceful co-existence. Once again, this is demonstrated in action when recently both leaders of Japan and South Korea Picked up the Drums to show case a cultural act with diplomatic significance.

When Leaders Pick Up the Drums: A New Rhythm for Japan–Korea Diplomacy

Diplomacy often advances not through formal communiqués but through moments that reveal shared humanity. In January 2026, such a moment occurred when Japanese Prime Minister Sanae Takaichi and South Korean President Lee Jae-myung sat side by side behind drum kits and performed K-pop hits following their bilateral summit in Nara, Japan (CBS News, 2026). Far from trivial, this was a cultural act with diplomatic significance.

During their summit, the two leaders—wearing matching blue athletic jackets—played BTS's "Dynamite" and "Golden" from K-Pop Demon Hunters, creating a viral moment that captured global attention. The performance was arranged after Prime Minister Takaichi recalled that President Lee had once mentioned learning the drums as a lifelong dream. Takaichi, a former university heavy-metal drummer, even coached him through the session. President Lee later joked about their differing skill levels but emphasized that Japan and South Korea had learned to "adjust to one another's rhythm," drawing a parallel between the drumming and their evolving diplomatic relationship.

Why This Moment Matters for Diplomacy:

1. Rhythm as a Metaphor for Cooperation

Drumming requires listening, adaptation, and synchronization—the same competencies essential for effective diplomacy. The shared beat symbolized a willingness to move forward together.

2. **Cultural Expression Softens Historical Tension**

   Despite long-standing grievances, cultural exchange creates emotional proximity that formal negotiations alone cannot achieve. The duet demonstrated to citizens that cooperation is not only possible but already unfolding in visible, human ways.

3. **A Public Gesture of Trust**

Drumming is vulnerable and unscripted. By engaging in this shared cultural practice, both leaders signaled openness and trust—qualities vital for sustaining diplomatic progress.

4. **A New Diplomatic Language**

Images of the two leaders drumming spread rapidly across global media, reframing the narrative from tension to creativity, partnership, and cultural respect.

The Larger Picture: Diplomacy Needs More Rhythm

The 2026 drumming moment underscores that cultural diplomacy is not a peripheral gesture but a strategic asset. Shared cultural practices generate emotional resonance that can stabilize political agreements. Drumming, in particular, embodies synchrony, mutual listening, shared energy, and visible commitment—qualities diplomacy often lacks. It reminds us that diplomacy is not only about interests; it is fundamentally about connection.

The Absence of Moral Imagination:

Diplomacy has become reactive rather than visionary. We respond to crises, but we rarely imagine futures. Moral imagination—the ability to envision a world better than the one we inherited—is the missing compass of global affairs. Without imagination, diplomacy becomes a management exercise. With imagination, it becomes a transformative force. The great diplomatic breakthroughs of history were not born from perfect conditions; they were born from leaders who dared to imagine what did not yet exist. Today, we need that courage more than ever.

A diplomat without moral imagination is like a navigator without a horizon. They may know the mechanics of steering, but they cannot chart a meaningful course. Moral imagination is the discipline of seeing beyond the immediate, of refusing to be imprisoned by the limitations of the present. It is the courage to propose what others dismiss as impossible, and the humility to recognize that every lasting peace begins as an act of creative audacity. When leaders dare to imagine, they do not escape reality—they expand it.

The absence of moral imagination has left global affairs trapped in a cycle of short-termism. We patch wounds instead of healing them; we manage tensions instead of transforming them. But diplomacy worthy of its name must be more than crisis containment. It must be the architecture of possibility. Moral imagination invites us to ask not only What is? but What could be? It challenges nations to rise above fear-driven politics and to invest in futures where cooperation is not an exception but a norm. In this sense, imagination is not a luxury—it is a responsibility.

And so, the call for moral imagination is a call for leadership that is both principled and bold. Leaders who cultivate this faculty do not wait for perfect conditions; they create conditions in which peace can take root. They understand that the future is not inherited—it is constructed. Today, in a world saturated with complexity and fatigue, moral imagination is the rarest form of courage. Yet it is precisely the courage our era demands if diplomacy is to reclaim its highest purpose: not merely to prevent catastrophe, but to illuminate a path toward a more humane and harmonious world.

The Overreliance on Power, and the Underinvestment in Understanding:

Power can coerce, but it cannot connect. It can enforce agreements, but it cannot inspire cooperation. Understanding, on the other hand, builds bridges that power alone cannot sustain. Diplomacy today is saturated with metrics of strength—military budgets, economic leverage, political alliances. Yet the most enduring diplomatic achievements have come from those who invested in understanding: understanding cultures, understanding histories, understanding the emotional landscapes of nations.

Before a nation can be influenced, it must first be understood. Understanding is not a courtesy; it is the first discipline of diplomacy. It is the quiet work that precedes every meaningful negotiation—the listening, the observing, the willingness to see the world through another's eyes. When diplomats rush to assert power without first cultivating understanding, they mistake dominance for leadership. True leadership begins not with the projection of strength, but with the humility to learn.

Understanding must come before strategy, before policy, before any attempt to shape outcomes. Without it, power becomes clumsy—an instrument wielded without insight. But when understanding leads, power becomes purposeful. It becomes the means through which shared interests are discovered rather than imposed. Nations that invest in understanding do not merely avoid conflict; they create the conditions for cooperation to flourish. They recognize that the emotional and cultural foundations of a society are not obstacles to diplomacy—they are its entry points.

And so, the imbalance between power and understanding is not simply a philosophical concern; it is a practical failure of modern statecraft. A diplomacy obsessed with power will always be reactive, brittle, and short-lived. A diplomacy grounded in understanding becomes resilient, adaptive, and humane. The future of global relations will belong to those who grasp this truth: that understanding is not the soft alternative to power—it is the force that gives power meaning, direction, and legitimacy.

The Neglect of the Human Spirit:

Perhaps the greatest absence in diplomacy today is the recognition of the human spirit. We speak of national interests, but rarely of national hopes. We speak of stability, but rarely of meaning. We speak of peace, but rarely of purpose.

Diplomacy must return to its humanistic roots. It must remember that peace is not merely the absence of war; it is the presence of dignity, opportunity, and mutual respect.

Cultural diplomacy, when practiced authentically, nurtures these conditions. It reminds us that humanity is not a geopolitical category—it is a shared inheritance.

A diplomacy that forgets the human spirit becomes a diplomacy without soul. Nations are not machines; they are living communities shaped by longing, memory, and aspiration. When diplomats fail to acknowledge the spiritual dimension of human life—the yearning for belonging, the desire for recognition, the quest for meaning—they negotiate only with the shell of a society, never its essence. The human spirit is not an abstraction; it is the quiet force that animates every struggle for justice, every movement for freedom, every dream of a better tomorrow.

The neglect of the human spirit has led to agreements that are technically sound yet emotionally hollow. Policies crafted without regard for human dignity may endure on paper, but they rarely endure in practice. Diplomacy must therefore reclaim its moral vocation: to uplift, to heal, to inspire. When cultural diplomacy is embraced not as performance but as practice, it becomes a conduit for empathy and a catalyst for reconciliation. It reminds us that beneath every border lies a human heartbeat, and beneath every negotiation lies a shared longing for a life of meaning.

And so, the future of diplomacy depends on our willingness to honor the human spirit as the central pillar of peace. When leaders recognize that people do not live by security alone—but by purpose, by connection, by the affirmation of their humanity—then diplomacy becomes more than a strategic exercise. It becomes a form of stewardship. It becomes the art of cultivating conditions in which individuals and nations alike can flourish. In this sense, the human spirit is not peripheral to diplomacy; it is its most enduring source of strength.

Policy Recommendation: Cultivating Human-Centered Diplomacy in Leadership Training

Re-Humanizing diplomatic leadership requires: Integration of Cultural Literacy in formal education, Creative Industry Engagement, and Public Dialogue into Diplomatic Training.

To prepare future leaders for the complexities of global diplomacy, training programs must move beyond technocratic expertise and incorporate humanistic competencies. This includes deep engagement with cultural diplomacy, the creative industries, and public dialogue. These domains are not peripheral—they are strategic assets that foster trust, emotional resonance, and sustainable cooperation.

Governments, foreign ministries, international institutions, and higher education should establish a Human-Centered Diplomacy Track within diplomatic academies and leadership development programs. This track should include:

1. **Cultural Literacy and Historical Empathy Modules:**

- Teach diplomats to interpret cultural symbols, rituals, and narratives as strategic intelligence.
- Include case studies like the Japan–South Korea cultural thaw (1998–2004) and the 2026 drumming summit as models of emotional diplomacy.

- Require immersive study of regional histories, literature, and artistic traditions to foster contextual sensitivity.

2. Creative Industry Engagement Practicum:

- Partner with artists, filmmakers, musicians, and designers to explore how cultural production shapes public sentiment, local and international perception.
- Train diplomats to collaborate with cultural ambassadors and creative professionals in shaping national image and soft power initiatives.
- Include workshops on cultural event planning, symbolic gestures, and media storytelling.

3. Public Dialogue and Emotional Intelligence Training:

- Equip leaders with tools for listening, dialogue facilitation, and narrative framing.

- Use role-play, theatre, and storytelling techniques to simulate high-stakes negotiations with emotional and cultural nuance.
- Encourage public-facing diplomacy through town halls, cultural festivals, and digital engagement platforms.

Implementation Strategy:

- ✓ Embed this track within existing diplomatic academies and foreign service institutes.
- ✓ Offer joint certification with cultural institutions, universities, and creative industry councils.
- ✓ Evaluate success through longitudinal studies on diplomatic outcomes, public trust metrics, and cross-cultural cooperation indices.

Diplomacy must evolve from a contest of interests to a choreography of understanding. Training future leaders to engage with culture, creativity, and public sentiment is not idealism—it is strategic foresight. A diplomacy that listens, feels, and imagines is a diplomacy that endures.

Final Invocation: Re-Humanize Diplomacy:

In closing, what is missing in diplomacy today is not knowledge, but wisdom. Not treaties, but trust. Not communication, but soulful connection.

Diplomacy must rediscover its cultural dimension, its empathic core, and its moral imagination. It must once again become a dialogue of civilizations rather than a contest of interests. Only then can it fulfill its highest purpose: not to manage the world as it is, but to guide the world toward what it can become. To re-humanize diplomacy is to recognize that global affairs are ultimately shaped by the interior lives of people—their values, their memories, their sense of belonging. When diplomacy acknowledges this inner terrain, it gains access to forms of influence that cannot be measured in conventional metrics. It becomes capable of healing historical wounds, not merely containing them. It becomes a space where nations can articulate not only what they fear, but what they hope for. This shift does not weaken diplomacy; it strengthens it by grounding it in the realities that truly move societies.

Re-humanizing diplomacy also requires a new kind of leadership—one that is willing to cultivate patience, curiosity, and moral clarity in an age dominated by speed and spectacle. Such leadership understands that durable peace is not engineered through pressure alone, but through the slow, deliberate work of building understanding and restoring dignity. When leaders choose to engage with one another not only as representatives of states but as custodians of human possibility, diplomacy becomes more than a tool of statecraft. It becomes a form of stewardship for the shared future of humanity.

References:

CBS News. (2026). Japanese and South Korean leaders bang out surprise K-pop drum duet. https://www.cbsnews.com/news/japan-south-korea-leaders-lee-jae-myung-sanae-takaichi-play-drums/

Cho, H. (2016). Cultural flows and regional reconciliation in East Asia. Seoul University Press.

Iwabuchi, K. (2015). Resilient borders and cultural diversity: Internationalism, brand nationalism, and multiculturalism in Japan. Lexington Books.

Kim, S. (2005). Cultural exchange and political rapprochement in Northeast Asia. Journal of Asian Studies, 64(3), 589–612.

Lee, J. (2012). Soft power and reconciliation: The Japan–Korea cultural opening. International Relations Review, 18(2), 45–62.

Obuchi, K., & Kim, D. (1998). Japan–Republic of Korea Joint Declaration: A New Japan–Republic of Korea Partnership towards the Twenty-first Century. Government of Japan.

Yoon, K. (2014). Transnational media consumption and youth identity in East Asia. Media, Culture & Society, 36(1), 45–60.

"The neglect of the human spirit has led to agreements that are technically sound, yet emotionally hollow."

Mosi Dorbayani

Briefing 10.

CULTURAL DIPLOMACY IN THE AGE OF AI: AI'S IMPACT ON CULTURAL IDENTITY AND PUBLIC DIALOGUE

In Brief:

In recent years, I have observed a profound shift in the way cultures communicate, interact, and even imagine themselves. We have entered an age in which artificial intelligence and algorithmic systems increasingly mediate our encounters with the world. This new reality brings remarkable opportunities for cultural exchange, yet it also presents unprecedented challenges to the integrity of cultural identity and the quality of public dialogue.

As a policy architect, scholar and songwriter who has long advocated for the centrality of culture in diplomacy, I now find myself compelled to address a new dimension of this work: the cultural consequences of AI-driven information ecosystems.

The stakes are high because the health of any civic society depends on the integrity of its shared narratives—those stories, symbols, and reference points through which people understand themselves and one another. When algorithmic systems shape these narratives through opaque curation, amplification, or suppression, they influence not only what individuals know but how they come to trust, empathize, and participate in collective life. Discussing these consequences is therefore essential to safeguarding the conditions that allow democratic discourse, cultural plurality, and social cohesion to flourish. Without such vigilance, societies risk drifting into fragmented realities where common ground becomes increasingly difficult to sustain.

This conversation is equally critical for international relations, where cultural understanding has long served as a stabilizing force amid political and economic tensions. AI-mediated information flows now shape how nations perceive each other, how cultural expressions circulate across borders, and how diplomatic intentions are interpreted—or misinterpreted. If left unexamined, these systems can distort cultural signals, exacerbate misunderstandings, and weaken the very foundations of soft power and cultural diplomacy. By confronting these dynamics directly, we strengthen the possibility of a global order in which technology supports, rather than undermines, mutual respect, cultural continuity, and constructive engagement among states.

AI as a New Cultural Actor:

Artificial intelligence is no longer a neutral tool. It has become a cultural actor—one that shapes narratives, amplifies certain voices, and silences others. It curates what we see, what we hear, and increasingly, what we believe. In doing so, AI influences the very fabric of cultural identity.

Cultures have always evolved, but today they evolve at a pace dictated not by communities themselves, but by the logic of algorithms. This raises a critical question: Who is the custodian of cultural truth when machines mediate our collective memory?

The urgency of this question becomes clear when we consider how civic well-being depends on shared meaning. A society's capacity to deliberate, to empathize, and to imagine a common future rests on the stability of its cultural reference points. When AI systems distort or fragment those reference points—whether through personalization, bias, or sheer velocity—they reshape the conditions under which citizens understand themselves and each other. Examining these consequences is therefore not optional; it is foundational to preserving the psychological and cultural infrastructure that allows civic life to remain coherent, participatory, and humane.

Moreover, the cultural effects of AI extend far beyond individual experience. They influence how communities form, how public trust is built or eroded, and how collective memory is constructed. When algorithmic systems privilege sensationalism over nuance or speed over reflection, they can weaken the very practices that sustain democratic culture: critical inquiry, respectful disagreement, and the slow work of consensus-building. Addressing these dynamics is essential if we are to ensure that technological innovation strengthens, rather than destabilizes, the social fabric.

On the international stage, the cultural role of AI carries profound diplomatic implications. Nations increasingly encounter one another not through direct cultural exchange but through algorithmically filtered representations—

images, narratives, and signals that may or may not reflect lived realities. Misperceptions can calcify quickly in such environments, shaping foreign policy attitudes, fueling cultural misunderstandings, and complicating efforts at cooperation. By scrutinizing how AI mediates cross-cultural perception, we safeguard the possibility of diplomacy grounded in authenticity, mutual respect, and informed engagement rather than in distortion or digital echo chambers.

The Erosion of Shared Realities:

Misinformation, accelerated by AI, fractures the shared realities that societies depend upon. When truth becomes negotiable and narratives become weaponized, cultural diplomacy faces a new and formidable adversary: the engineered distortion of public consciousness.

I have always believed that dialogue is the cornerstone of peaceful coexistence. Yet dialogue becomes impossible when citizens no longer inhabit the same informational universe. In such a climate, cultural diplomacy must evolve from facilitating exchange to safeguarding the conditions that make exchange possible.

This erosion of shared realities has profound implications for civic well-being. A society cannot function when its members operate from incompatible understandings of basic facts, values, or intentions. AI-driven misinformation exploits cognitive vulnerabilities, accelerates polarization, and undermines the trust that binds communities together. Addressing these dynamics is not merely a matter of correcting falsehoods; it is about protecting the psychological and cultural foundations that enable people to recognize one another as participants in a common civic project.

The consequences extend beyond domestic cohesion. When algorithmic systems distort public perception, they also distort how societies interpret the actions, cultures, and motivations of others. Misunderstandings that once took years to develop can now be manufactured in hours, shaping public sentiment and influencing policy decisions before diplomatic channels have a chance to respond. In this environment, cultural diplomacy must take on a new role: not only fostering mutual understanding, but actively countering the forces that seek to fragment it.

Ultimately, the challenge is not simply technological but profoundly human. AI-mediated misinformation exploits the emotional and cultural fault lines that already exist within and between societies. If left unaddressed, these fractures can calcify into hostility, suspicion, and disengagement—conditions that make cooperation nearly impossible. By confronting the cultural dimensions of this problem, we reaffirm the essential truth that diplomacy begins not with institutions, but with people who share enough reality to imagine a future together.

Cultural Identity in Flux:

AI's influence on identity is subtle but profound. It shapes how individuals perceive their own culture and how they interpret the cultures of others. It can reinforce stereotypes or dismantle them; it can preserve heritage or dilute it. The outcome depends not on the technology itself, but on the values embedded within it.

I often remind decision-makers, my peer scholars and students that cultural identity is not a static artifact—it is a living, breathing expression of human experience. But when identity is filtered through algorithmic preferences, it risks becoming a commodity rather than a heritage.

This is especially concerning because cultural identity is among the most sensitive dimensions of human life. It carries memory, belonging, and meaning; it anchors individuals within communities and communities within history. When AI systems intervene in this domain—whether by curating cultural content, shaping linguistic norms, or influencing aesthetic preferences—they do so with a power that can unintentionally destabilize the very foundations of personal and collective identity. Such influence must be handled with extraordinary care, for once cultural harm occurs, it is often irreversible.

Moreover, the rapid pace of algorithmic mediation can create a dissonance between inherited traditions and digitally accelerated cultural shifts. Communities may find themselves struggling to reconcile long-standing practices with the identities being subtly shaped by AI-driven environments. This tension can generate confusion, alienation, or even cultural loss, particularly among younger generations whose sense of self is formed in digital spaces. Recognizing these risks is essential if we are to ensure that technological innovation does not erode the continuity and dignity of cultural heritage.

The stakes are even higher in multicultural societies, where the delicate balance between diverse identities depends on mutual respect and accurate representation. When AI systems misinterpret, flatten, or exoticize cultural expressions, they can inadvertently reinforce harmful narratives or deepen social divides. Protecting cultural identity from such distortions is not merely a matter of ethics; it is a matter of social stability. A society that mishandles cultural identity places its cohesion at risk.

Ultimately, the question is not whether AI will influence cultural identity—it already does—but whether we will guide that influence with responsibility, humility, and foresight. Cultural identity deserves the highest degree of protection because it shapes how people understand themselves and how they relate to others. If we fail to safeguard this sensitive terrain, we risk allowing technology to reshape humanity in ways that diminish our diversity, our memory, and our shared humanity.

A Call for Ethical Cultural Stewardship:

In this age of digital acceleration, cultural diplomacy must assume a new responsibility: to advocate for ethical AI that respects cultural diversity, protects human dignity, and promotes truthful dialogue.

We must encourage governments, institutions, and technology developers to recognize that cultural ecosystems are as fragile as natural ones. They require stewardship, not exploitation. They require transparency, not manipulation. And above all, they require a commitment to the human spirit that no machine can replicate.

This responsibility becomes even more urgent when we acknowledge that cultural harm is not easily repaired. Once a tradition is misrepresented, a narrative distorted, or a community's identity reduced to an algorithmic caricature, the damage can echo across generations. Ethical cultural stewardship demands that we treat cultural expression with the same reverence we afford to historical sites or endangered languages. It requires us to ensure that AI systems do not merely process culture, but engage with it in ways that honor its depth, complexity, and humanity.

To achieve this, we must cultivate a global ethic that places cultural sensitivity at the center of technological design. This means involving cultural practitioners, scholars, and community leaders in the development of AI systems that touch public life. It means embedding safeguards that prevent the erasure of minority voices, the amplification of harmful stereotypes, or the commodification of sacred traditions. Ethical stewardship is not a technical add-on; it is a moral imperative that shapes how technology interacts with the human story.

Ultimately, the future of cultural diplomacy will depend on our willingness to defend the integrity of cultural identity in a world increasingly shaped by machines. If we fail to act, we risk allowing technology to reshape culture in ways that diminish its richness and diversity. But if we rise to the challenge, we can ensure that AI becomes a partner in cultural flourishing rather than a force of cultural erosion. The task before us is clear: to protect what is most human in us, even as we navigate the frontiers of the digital age.

Toward a More Conscious Digital Future:

I remain optimistic. AI, when guided by ethical principles and cultural sensitivity, can become a powerful ally. It can democratize access to culture, amplify marginalized voices, and foster global understanding on a scale previously unimaginable.

But this future will not emerge on its own. It must be shaped—deliberately, thoughtfully, and diplomatically.

As I reflect on the current world situation, I am convinced that cultural diplomacy has never been more essential. In an era where misinformation divides and algorithms influence identity, our task is clear: to ensure that humanity remains at the center of our technological evolution, and that culture continues to serve as a bridge rather than a battleground.

This requires a renewed commitment to intentionality. We must design digital spaces that cultivate reflection rather than reaction, curiosity rather than suspicion, and connection rather than fragmentation. A conscious digital future is one in which technology supports the flourishing of cultural diversity rather than reducing it to patterns of consumption. Such a future depends on our willingness to embed ethical guardrails into the very architecture of AI systems, ensuring that they elevate human understanding instead of eroding it.

Equally important is the cultivation of digital literacy as a form of cultural resilience. Citizens must be empowered to navigate algorithmic environments with discernment, to recognize when narratives are being manipulated, and to understand how their identities are being shaped by unseen forces. This is not merely a technical skill—it is a civic necessity. A society capable of interpreting its digital landscape is a society capable of protecting its cultural integrity.

Ultimately, the path toward a more conscious digital future is a collective endeavor. Governments, educators, cultural institutions, and technology developers must work together to ensure that AI strengthens the bonds between people rather than weakening them. If we succeed, we will not only safeguard cultural identity—we will expand the possibilities for human connection, creativity, and cooperation in ways that honor the richness of our shared humanity.

Establishing Relationship with AI:

Artists, writers, and the broader creative industry have a uniquely powerful role to play in shaping a healthier cultural relationship with AI. Their work reaches people not through policy or technical design, but through imagination, emotion, and meaning—the very spaces where cultural identity is formed and protected. Here are recommendations that speak directly to their strengths and responsibilities:

1. Reclaim Narrative Agency:

Creative practitioners can counterbalance algorithmic influence by producing work that resists simplification and challenges the homogenizing tendencies of AI-driven platforms.

➢ Craft stories, songs, and artworks that illuminate the complexity of human experience.
➢ Highlight perspectives that algorithms often overlook or misrepresent.
➢ Create narratives that remind audiences of the richness of cultural nuance, ambiguity, and contradiction—qualities machines struggle to capture.

By doing so, artists help ensure that cultural identity remains shaped by human intention rather than automated curation.

2. Model Ethical Engagement with Technology:

The creative sector can demonstrate how to use AI tools responsibly without surrendering artistic integrity.

✓ Experiment with AI as a collaborator rather than a replacement.

✓ Make transparent the processes behind AI-assisted work to demystify the technology.

✓ Advocate for ethical standards in creative AI tools, especially around consent, attribution, and cultural sensitivity.

This positions artists as cultural stewards who show society how to integrate technology without losing the human core of creativity.

3. Protect and Revitalize Cultural Memory:

Writers, musicians, filmmakers, and designers can help safeguard cultural heritage in an era when digital systems may distort or erase it.

✓ Document traditions, languages, and stories that risk being overshadowed by algorithmic trends.

✓ Use creative platforms to amplify marginalized cultural voices.

✓ Build archives, exhibitions, and performances that preserve cultural memory in forms resistant to algorithmic manipulation.

Their work becomes a living counter-archive—one that resists the flattening effects of automated systems.

4. Strengthen Public Imagination and Digital Literacy:

The creative industry can help audiences understand how AI shapes perception and identity.

➤ Produce works that explore the ethical, emotional, and cultural implications of AI.

➤ Use storytelling to make abstract technological issues accessible and relatable.

➤ Encourage critical thinking about digital environments through satire, speculative fiction, visual metaphor, and performance.

When people understand the forces shaping their informational world, they become more resilient to manipulation.

5. Serve as Cultural Diplomats in Their Own Right:

Artists and writers have always been ambassadors of cultural understanding. In the AI era, this role becomes even more vital.

✓ Participate in cross-cultural collaborations that model respectful exchange.

✓ Use creative work to bridge divides exacerbated by misinformation.

✓ Engage in international dialogues where cultural expression becomes a tool for peacebuilding and mutual recognition.

Their contributions help ensure that culture remains a bridge—never a battleground.

The Role of Governments: What Needs to Be Done

1. Establish Robust Regulatory Frameworks to Protect Creators and Cultural Integrity:

Governments must enact clear, enforceable laws that regulate how AI systems interact with creative content and cultural expression. This includes requiring transparency in how AI models are trained, mandating consent for the use of artistic works in datasets, and ensuring that creators retain control over how their intellectual property is reproduced, transformed, or monetized. Such regulation is not merely a matter of economic fairness—it is a cultural safeguard. When artists and cultural practitioners lose ownership of their work, societies risk losing the authenticity and diversity that underpin cultural identity itself.

By protecting creators through strong legal frameworks, governments help maintain the integrity of cultural ecosystems in the digital age. These protections also serve as a stabilizing force in international relations. When nations respect one another's cultural assets and uphold shared standards for intellectual property, they reduce the likelihood of cultural exploitation and foster an environment where cultural exchange is grounded in trust, reciprocity, and mutual respect. In this way, IP protection becomes a diplomatic tool—one that supports peace by affirming the dignity of each nation's cultural heritage.

2. Strengthen International Intellectual Property Agreements to Promote Cultural Diplomacy and Global Understanding:

Governments should work collaboratively to modernize international IP treaties so they reflect the realities of AI-driven creation and distribution. This includes harmonizing standards for digital rights management, establishing cross-border mechanisms for enforcing creator protections, and developing shared ethical guidelines for the use of cultural data in AI systems. Such cooperation ensures that artists and creative industries are protected not only within their own borders but across the global digital landscape.

Stronger international IP agreements also contribute directly to peacebuilding and diplomatic stability. When nations recognize and protect each other's cultural expressions, they affirm the principle that culture is not a resource to be extracted but a heritage to be honored. This mutual recognition reduces cultural tensions, counters the weaponization of misinformation, and creates pathways for dialogue even in times of political strain. In this sense, intellectual property rights become more than legal instruments—they become instruments of understanding, enabling nations to engage with one another through respect for the creative contributions that define their identities.

Culture as the First Bridge: A Reflection on Diplomacy in the Age of AI

Cultural diplomacy, to me, has always been an act of faith—faith in the idea that culture carries truths that politics alone cannot articulate. Throughout my life as a cultural diplomat and songwriter, I have witnessed how a single melody, a song, a poem, or a shared story can open doors that formal negotiations struggle to unlock. Culture softens the ground on which dialogue can grow. It reminds us that before we are citizens of nations, we are human beings shaped by memory, meaning, and emotion. In this sense, cultural diplomacy is not merely a profession; it is a calling to elevate the human spirit in places where misunderstanding and mistrust often prevail.

In today's world, where digital acceleration reshapes how people perceive themselves and one another, the work of cultural diplomacy has become even more vital. I have long argued that culture is the heartbeat of international relations, and now that heartbeat is mediated by algorithms that do not feel, do not empathize, and do not understand the sacredness of identity. This is why we must be vigilant. When culture becomes distorted, commodified, or manipulated, the consequences ripple far beyond the arts— they affect social cohesion, civic well-being, and the fragile architecture of peace. My task, as I see it, is to advocate for a world in which technology serves culture, not the other way around.

Yet despite the challenges, I remain profoundly hopeful. I have seen how artists, educators, diplomats, and communities can rise to protect what is most human in us. Cultural diplomacy gives us the tools to bridge divides, to restore shared realities, and to remind nations that peace is not built solely through treaties but through understanding.

As I reflect on the path ahead, I am convinced that our greatest responsibility is to ensure that culture continues to illuminate our common humanity. In doing so, we safeguard not only our identities, but the possibility of a more compassionate and cooperative world.

In Closing:

As I look across the landscape we are shaping—through culture, through technology, through the choices we make as societies—I am reminded that our greatest responsibility is not simply to innovate, but to safeguard what makes us human. Cultural diplomacy teaches us that identity, memory, and meaning are not abstractions; they are living forces that guide how we relate to one another and how we imagine our shared future. In this moment of rapid transformation, we must hold fast to the principle that culture is not a by-product of progress, but its compass.

The rise of AI has brought extraordinary possibilities, yet it has also revealed how fragile our cultural ecosystems truly are. If we are careless, we risk allowing algorithms to shape the stories we tell, the values we uphold, and the identities we pass on to future generations. But if we act with intention—through ethical stewardship, thoughtful regulation, and a renewed commitment to cultural understanding—we can ensure that technology becomes a partner in human flourishing rather than a force of erosion. Ultimately, the work ahead calls for courage, imagination, and diplomacy in equal measure. It asks us to protect the dignity of creators, to honor the diversity of cultures, and to insist that humanity remains at the center of every technological horizon we pursue. If we rise to that challenge, we will not only preserve the richness of our cultural identities—we will strengthen the foundations of peace, empathy, and cooperation that bind us together as a global community.

"Power can coerce, but it cannot connect. It can enforce agreements, but it cannot inspire cooperation."

Mosi Dorbayani

Briefing 11.

ADAPTIVE CROSS-CULTURAL NEGOTIATION: THE DIAGNOSTIC FOUNDATIONS IN DIPLOMACY

In Brief:

Cross-cultural negotiation in diplomacy begins long before parties sit at a table. It begins in the quiet work of reading cultural signals, discerning how a counterpart understands hierarchy, time, obligation, and the very meaning of agreement. In diplomatic settings, these elements are not peripheral; they are the negotiation. A negotiator who assumes universality—who treats directness, speed, or contractual precision as neutral norms—will misread the room and misinterpret intent. By contrast, a culturally attuned negotiator recognizes that every diplomatic exchange is shaped by inherited narratives, collective memory, and the symbolic weight of gestures. This introduction frames negotiation not as a contest of positions, but as a disciplined act of cultural interpretation.

A diagnostic for cultural negotiation styles helps practitioners avoid the trap of projecting their own norms onto others. Such a diagnostic typically examines four dimensions: communication style (direct–indirect), power distance (egalitarian–hierarchical), orientation to time (linear–cyclical), and approach to agreement (contractual–

relational). When applied thoughtfully, it reveals why a counterpart may avoid saying "no," why silence may signal respect rather than resistance, or why a seemingly minor procedural detail carries deep symbolic meaning. Diplomats who use this diagnostic do not stereotype; they use it to slow their assumptions, to ask better questions, and to recognize when a negotiation is actually occurring in the subtext rather than the spoken text.

Diagnostic Foundations for the Adaptive Negotiator:

A diagnostic for cultural negotiation styles is not a static chart of traits; it is a living instrument in the hands of an adaptive negotiator. Its purpose is not to categorize people, but to illuminate the cultural logic that shapes how meaning is conveyed, how authority is expressed, and how agreement is signaled. An adaptive negotiator approaches this diagnostic with humility, recognizing that culture is not a costume worn by the other party—it is a framework that shapes one's own assumptions just as powerfully. By examining dimensions such as communication style, hierarchy, time orientation, and relational expectations, the negotiator becomes aware of the invisible architecture of the conversation. This awareness is the first act of adaptation: the shift from assuming universality to recognizing plurality.

Communication style is often the most visible dimension, yet it is also the most frequently misinterpreted. Cultures that value directness may see clarity as respect, while cultures that favor indirectness may view subtlety as diplomacy. An adaptive negotiator uses the diagnostic to read these cues without judgment. When faced with indirect communication, they do not push for premature clarity; they listen for what is implied, observe what is left unsaid, and allow space for meaning to emerge. When engaging with direct communicators, they match the clarity without mistaking it for aggression. Adaptation here is not mimicry—it is alignment. It is the disciplined choice to communicate in a way that honors the counterpart's cultural expectations while maintaining one's own integrity.

Power distance and time orientation add deeper layers to the diagnostic. In hierarchical cultures, authority may be centralized, and decisions may require ritual, consultation, or symbolic gestures. An adaptive negotiator recognizes that pressing for immediate commitments in such contexts is not strategic—it is culturally tone-deaf. They adjust by identifying the true decision-makers, respecting protocol, and pacing the negotiation in a way that aligns with the counterpart's internal processes. Similarly, time orientation—whether linear and efficiency-driven or cyclical and relationship-centered—shapes how progress is perceived. The adaptive negotiator uses the diagnostic to recalibrate expectations: in some cultures, a slower pace is not resistance but respect; in others, speed signals competence. Adaptation means shifting one's tempo without losing one's direction.

The relational dimension is where the diagnostic becomes most transformative. Some cultures treat negotiation as a transaction; others treat it as a relationship-building ritual in which trust precedes substance. An adaptive negotiator reads this early and adjusts accordingly. If the counterpart values relational depth, the negotiator invests in rapport, shared experiences, and symbolic gestures before discussing terms. If the counterpart prioritizes efficiency, the negotiator moves swiftly to structure and clarity. This is the essence of adaptive negotiation: the ability to shift posture, pace, and process in response to cultural signals. The diagnostic is not a checklist—it is a compass. It guides the negotiator toward choices that reduce friction, enhance mutual understanding, and create the conditions for durable agreement.

Decision tree for adaptive cross-cultural tactics:

A decision tree for adapting tactics begins with a simple, disciplined question: What is the cultural logic shaping this interaction? Building on the diagnostic, the adaptive negotiator does not move directly to offers and counter-offers; they first decide how to engage. The tree starts with observable cues—communication style, hierarchy, time orientation, and relational emphasis—and then guides the negotiator toward specific tactical choices. Each branch is a reminder that there is no single "best" tactic; there is only a tactic that is more or less aligned with the counterpart's cultural expectations. The decision tree therefore functions as a practical bridge between cultural insight and behavioral adjustment.

The first branch concerns communication style. If the counterpart appears direct, the negotiator can safely use explicit language, clear proposals, and open disagreement. If the counterpart appears indirect, the negotiator shifts to exploratory questions, softer phrasing, and greater attention to non-verbal cues and context. The second branch addresses power distance.

In egalitarian settings, it is usually appropriate to engage multiple stakeholders, invite open discussion, and expect visible participation from all. In hierarchical settings, the negotiator must identify the key authority figures, respect protocol, and avoid forcing public commitments from those who are not empowered to decide.

Each of these branches leads to different tactical choices about who to address, how to phrase requests, and when to press for clarity.

The next branches focus on time orientation and relational emphasis. If the culture is time-efficient and linear, the negotiator can move relatively quickly to agenda, structure, and concrete outcomes, signaling respect by being concise and prepared. If the culture is time-flexible or cyclical, the negotiator slows the pace, allows for pauses, and recognizes that apparent "delay" may be part of a legitimate decision rhythm.

Similarly, if the counterpart is transaction-focused, the negotiator emphasizes terms, performance, and measurable benefits. If the counterpart is relationship-focused, the negotiator invests in trust-building activities, symbolic gestures, and shared narratives before expecting firm commitments. At each node, the adaptive negotiator asks: Given what I see, which path honors their logic while still serving our objectives?

The following is an illustration of Decision Tree for Apapting Tactics:

Decision Tree for Adapting Tactics

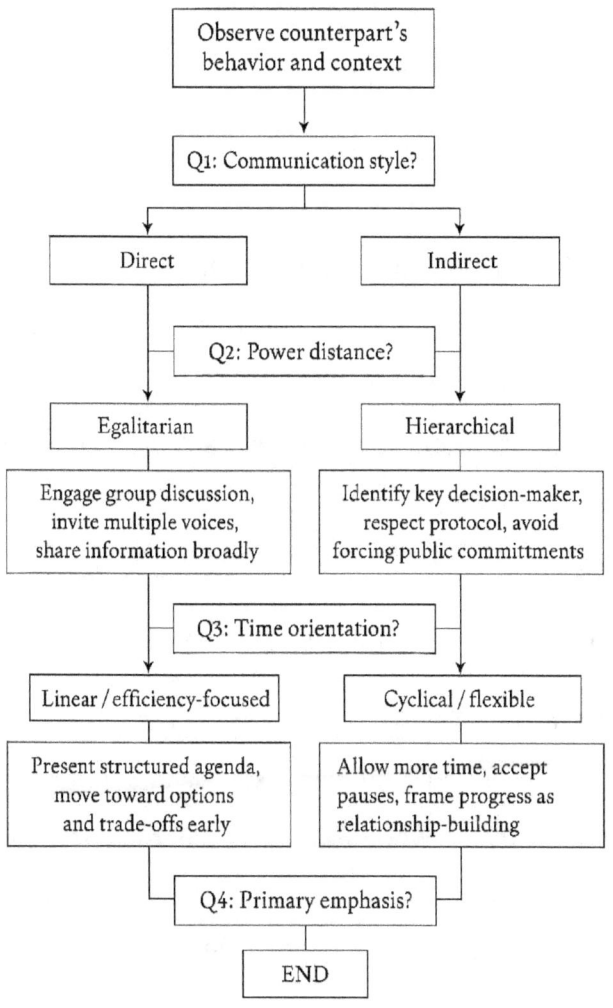

Observe counterpart's behavior and context

Q1: Communication style?

Direct | Indirect

Q2: Power distance?

Egalitarian | Hierarchical

Engage group discussion, invite multiple voices, share information broadly | Identify key decision-maker, respect protocol, avoid forcing public committments

Q3: Time orientation?

Linear / efficiency-focused | Cyclical / flexible

Present structured agenda, move toward options and trade-offs early | Allow more time, accept pauses, frame progress as relationship-building

Q4: Primary emphasis?

END

In practice, the adaptive negotiator does not walk through this tree mechanically; they internalize it as a mental model. They may start at any node—perhaps noticing hierarchy first, or time orientation—then quickly trace the implications for tone, pacing, and process. The power of the decision tree lies in its discipline: it prevents the negotiator from defaulting to their own cultural habits and calling them "neutral." Instead, it prompts deliberate, context-sensitive choices. Over time, this structured adaptability becomes second nature, enabling the negotiator to move fluidly across cultures while maintaining clarity of purpose and respect for difference.

Adaptive Tactics in Cross-cultural Practice:

Applied cross-culture is the field where theory meets practice—where cultural diagnostics, adaptive tactics, and negotiation frameworks are not merely studied but deployed in real-world settings. In the context of diplomacy, applied cross-culture demands more than awareness; it requires operational fluency. The adaptive negotiator becomes a practitioner of cultural logic, using tools like diagnostics and decision trees not as academic exercises but as instruments of influence, trust-building, and resolution. Each negotiation becomes a site of cultural application, where the negotiator must read, respond, and recalibrate in real time.

The diagnostic for cultural negotiation styles is a cornerstone of applied cross-culture. It translates abstract cultural dimensions into actionable insights: how to speak, when to pause, whom to address, and what signals to interpret. In applied settings, this diagnostic is not used in isolation—it is embedded in briefing protocols, stakeholder mapping, and pre-negotiation strategy. For example, a diplomat preparing for a multilateral climate negotiation might use the diagnostic to anticipate which delegations will value relational trust over technical precision, or which will require hierarchical deference before substantive dialogue. Applied cross-culture turns these insights into strategic posture.

The decision tree for adapting tactics is where applied cross-culture becomes dynamic. It enables the negotiator to shift tactics midstream—responding to indirect cues, adjusting pace, or reframing proposals based on cultural feedback. In practice, this means knowing when to switch from distributive bargaining to integrative dialogue, when to defer to seniority, and when to signal commitment through symbolic acts rather than contractual language. The decision tree is not just a planning tool; it is a live instrument of adaptation. In applied cross-culture, it is taught through simulations, role-plays, and post-negotiation debriefs, ensuring that the negotiator internalizes its logic.

In Closing:

The practice of cross-cultural negotiation in diplomacy is not a matter of technique alone—it is a matter of disposition. The adaptive negotiator does not merely learn cultural frameworks; they cultivate a posture of listening, humility, and strategic empathy. They understand that every negotiation is shaped by inherited meanings, and that success often depends not on persuasion, but on recognition. Applied cross-culture transforms this understanding into action, equipping negotiators to operate across difference with precision and grace.

The diagnostic for cultural negotiation styles offers a structured way to perceive the invisible: how communication, hierarchy, time, and trust shape the rhythm and meaning of diplomatic exchange. But perception is not enough. The decision tree for adapting tactics turns insight into movement, guiding the negotiator through real-time choices that honor the counterpart's cultural logic while advancing shared goals. These tools are not static—they evolve with each encounter, each reflection, each moment of recalibration.

Applied cross-culture is the field where these tools are tested, refined, and embodied. It is where diplomats, mediators, and leaders learn to read silence as signal, to see ritual as negotiation, and to treat adaptation not as compromise but as competence. In this field, case studies become mirrors, revealing how cultural framing altered outcomes and how adaptive choices created space for resolution. The work is not only strategic—it is ethical. It affirms that respect for cultural difference is not a barrier to agreement, but its foundation.

Ultimately, cross-cultural negotiation in diplomacy is a discipline of alignment. It asks the negotiator to align their tactics with the counterpart's worldview, their pace with the counterpart's rhythm, and their purpose with the counterpart's values. In doing so, it transforms negotiation from a transactional act into a relational one—from a contest of positions into a shared search for meaning. This is the promise of applied cross-culture: that in the space between cultures, we can build agreements that endure.

Briefing 12.

POLICY IN A SHARED WORLD: ALIGNING NATIONS, ADVANCING HUMANITY

In Brief:

Policy, at its best, is not an exercise in asserting power but a disciplined practice of collective stewardship. Decisions that shape the public sphere demand more than swift declarations; they require time, consultation, and a willingness to understand the lived realities of those affected. When policymakers approach their work as a process of cultivation rather than command, they create space for nuance, dissent, and shared ownership. This shift from authority to responsibility transforms policy from a top-down directive into a collaborative social contract.

Such leadership begins with humility — the recognition that no individual, regardless of expertise or position, holds all the answers. Listening becomes an ethical act, a way of acknowledging the dignity and intelligence of the community. Clarity of thought follows from this openness, allowing leaders to distinguish between what is expedient and what is right. Moral courage then becomes the bridge between understanding and action, enabling policymakers to make choices that honor their implicit promise to society:

to safeguard the public good even when the path is complex or politically inconvenient.

Balancing pragmatism with vision is the hallmark of enduring policy leadership. Pragmatism ensures that decisions are grounded in evidence, feasibility, and the constraints of the present. Vision ensures that these decisions do not merely react to immediate pressures but contribute to a more just and humane future. When these two forces are held in productive tension, policy becomes a tool not only for solving problems but for elevating the human condition. It becomes a mechanism through which societies articulate who they are and who they aspire to become.

Ultimately, policies shaped by empathy, informed by knowledge, and guided by integrity transcend the bureaucratic machinery through which they are implemented. They become instruments of collective progress — frameworks that empower rather than restrict, that heal rather than divide. When leaders commit to this standard, policy ceases to be a distant administrative function and becomes a living expression of societal values. In this way, governance evolves from the management of systems to the cultivation of human flourishing.

Policy Decisions in Global Governance: Pragmatism Vs. Vision

Policy decisions in global governance function as the connective tissue between nations, institutions, and the shared aspirations of humanity. They are not merely administrative outputs but instruments through which the international community articulates its collective will. In the author's framing, global policy must rise above national posturing and become a disciplined practice of dialogue across cultures, economies, and political systems. When crafted with deliberation and respect, such decisions help stabilize an increasingly interdependent world, ensuring that cooperation prevails over fragmentation.

At the heart of effective global governance lies the moral responsibility of policymakers to listen — not only to states, but to peoples, communities, and the vulnerable voices often overshadowed by geopolitical interests. Humility becomes a diplomatic virtue, enabling leaders to recognize that global challenges cannot be solved through unilateral declarations. Whether addressing climate change, migration, public health, or digital ethics, clarity of thought and moral courage are essential. Each decision becomes a promise not just to one nation, but to the global public whose lives are shaped by these far-reaching choices.

The balance between pragmatism and vision is particularly vital on the world stage. Pragmatism ensures that global agreements are implementable, grounded in evidence, and sensitive to the diverse capacities of states. Vision ensures that these agreements do not merely manage crises but chart pathways toward a more sustainable future with equal opportunities. In the author's view, the global governance must be anticipatory rather than reactive — capable of uplifting the human condition across borders and generations. When this balance is achieved, policy becomes a catalyst for shared progress rather than a negotiation of competing interests.

Ultimately, policy decisions in global governance gain legitimacy when they are shaped by empathy, informed by rigorous knowledge, and guided by unwavering integrity. Such decisions transcend bureaucratic procedure and become expressions of humanity's highest values. They remind us that governance is not simply the management of systems, but the stewardship of a shared world. When global leaders embrace this ethos, policy becomes a bridge — linking nations, protecting dignity, and enabling collective flourishing in an era that demands nothing less.

Policy: A Bridge Linking Nations

A well-crafted policy does more than regulate behavior within a single state; it establishes shared expectations, shared language, and shared commitments. In a fragmented world, these common frameworks act like structural beams, allowing countries with different histories, cultures, and interests to meet on stable ground rather than in the volatility of ad-hoc negotiation.

Policies also link nations by transforming abstract global challenges into coordinated action. Climate agreements, trade standards, public-health protocols, and digital-ethics frameworks all illustrate this dynamic. No country can solve these issues alone, and unilateral action often produces uneven or counterproductive outcomes. When nations adopt policies that are harmonized, interoperable, or mutually reinforcing, they create a lattice of cooperation that strengthens the entire international system. The bridge, in this sense, is built from shared responsibility.

There is also a human dimension to this bridging function. Policies grounded in empathy and respect acknowledge that the consequences of global decisions are felt by real people — workers, families, migrants, students, communities. When policymakers honor this reality, they craft decisions that are not merely strategic but humane. This ethical orientation fosters trust between nations, because it signals that cooperation is not a zero-sum contest but a collective endeavor to safeguard dignity and opportunity across borders.

Finally, policy becomes a bridge when it is guided by integrity. Nations are more willing to collaborate when they believe their partners act with consistency, transparency, and moral courage. Integrity stabilizes expectations, reduces uncertainty, and allows long-term commitments to flourish. In the author's view, this is where policy transcends bureaucracy: it becomes a conduit through which nations can align their aspirations, reconcile their differences, and move together toward a more just and sustainable global future.

National Policy and International Community:

National policy aligns with the international community when a country understands itself not as an isolated actor but as a participant in a shared global ecosystem. Alignment begins with recognizing that many contemporary challenges — climate change, migration, digital governance, public health, trade — are inherently transnational. When national leaders frame their policies with this interdependence in mind, they naturally gravitate toward standards, norms, and cooperative mechanisms that reflect global expectations rather than purely domestic impulses.

This mindset shift is foundational: it transforms policy from a defensive posture to a collaborative contribution.

Alignment also occurs through deliberate engagement with international institutions and multilateral processes. When a nation participates actively in global forums, treaty bodies, and specialized agencies, it gains access to collective knowledge, best practices, and negotiated norms. These inputs help shape national legislation, regulatory frameworks, and administrative procedures.

The author often emphasizes that such engagement is not passive compliance but informed co-creation — a way for states to help shape the global agenda while ensuring their own policies remain coherent with international commitments.

Another pathway to alignment is the integration of international standards into domestic governance. This can take the form of harmonizing national laws with global conventions, adopting internationally recognized benchmarks, or embedding human-rights and sustainability principles into national planning. When states internalize these norms, they create policy environments that are interoperable with those of other nations. This reduces friction, enhances trust, and strengthens the predictability of international cooperation. It also signals that the nation sees itself as a responsible steward of shared global values.

Finally, alignment is sustained through ethical leadership — the willingness to act with integrity, transparency, and empathy in both domestic and international arenas.

When national policies are guided by principles that resonate globally, they become bridges rather than barriers.

They demonstrate that a country's pursuit of its own interests is compatible with the well-being of the wider world. In the author's view, this is yet again where national policy transcends its borders: it becomes a contribution to global governance, reinforcing the idea that progress is most durable when nations move not in isolation but in concert.

In Closing:

The alignment of national policy with the international community is ultimately an expression of shared responsibility in an interdependent world. When states craft their policies with awareness of global norms, ethical obligations, and the lived realities of people beyond their borders, they elevate governance from a domestic exercise to a contribution to collective stability. This is the spirit the author consistently highlights: the idea that nations strengthen themselves not by retreating inward, but by engaging outward with clarity, humility, and purpose. In doing so, they help build a global environment where cooperation is not an exception but a habit — a steady architecture of trust that supports peace, development, and human dignity.

Such alignment also reflects a deeper philosophical truth about governance in the twenty-first century: no nation's future is fully its own. The policies enacted within one jurisdiction ripple outward, shaping markets, ecosystems, and human mobility across continents. When national leaders embrace this reality, they begin to see policy not as a shield but as a bridge — a means of linking aspirations, harmonizing standards, and advancing shared progress. Let us remember that principled policymaking, grounded in empathy and integrity, is one of the most powerful tools humanity possesses for shaping a more just and sustainable global order.

For Further Insight and Practice:

"KNOWLEDGE IS POWER" IS A FALSE BELIEF!

In Brief:

The long-standing maxim "knowledge is power" has been widely accepted across academic, professional, and policy-making circles. Yet, despite unprecedented global access to higher education and the annual graduation of vast cohorts from the world's most prestigious universities, the correlation between knowledge and actual power remains tenuous. Many graduates—Harvard, Oxford, Cambridge, and others among them—enter the world equipped with credentials and intellectual capital, yet a significant proportion struggle to secure meaningful employment, influence, or agency. If knowledge alone were inherently powerful, the contemporary world, rich with educated individuals, would presumably exhibit far fewer systemic challenges.

Knowledge on Its Own Is Not Power!

This paradox invites a deeper examination of what knowledge represents and how it functions. Etymologically, the word knowledge contains know and edge, suggesting an orientation toward insight, discernment, and the cutting edge of innovation. Knowledge, therefore, offers a potential advantage—an "edge"—but potential is not synonymous with power. Power emerges only when knowledge is mobilized, directed, and sustained through purposeful action, which is enforced by determination and commitment. Therefore, "Knowledge Is Power" is a False Belief.

In my view and experience, a more accurate formulation of power is:

Power = Knowledge + Planning + Action × Determination and Commitment

This equation underscores that knowledge is merely the starting point. Planning provides direction, action converts intention into movement, and determination with commitment ensures continuity in the face of obstacles. Without these additional components, knowledge remains inert—valuable but unrealized.

The contemporary landscape offers countless examples of individuals with limited formal education who surpass highly credentialed peers in influence, innovation, and impact. Their success is not a repudiation of knowledge but a demonstration that applied knowledge—strategically organized and persistently executed—outperforms knowledge held passively.

Thus, knowledge becomes power only when it is intentionally applied toward a defined objective. When knowledge is integrated into a coherent plan, enacted through deliberate steps, and reinforced by sustained determination, it becomes transformative. It can reshape institutions, advance communities, and contribute meaningfully to societal progress.

In an era that often equates credentials with capability, this reframing is essential. The future of leadership and organizational development depends not merely on what individuals know, but on how effectively they convert knowledge into purposeful, committed action.

An Impressive Reservoir of Potential:

Knowledge in isolation is inert—an impressive reservoir of potential that remains dormant until it is directed with purpose. The world is full of individuals who possess remarkable intellectual capacity yet fail to translate that capacity into meaningful influence. What separates those who merely know from those who achieve is not the volume of information they hold, but the clarity of their aim and the discipline with which they pursue it. Knowledge must be mobilized, not admired; it must be put to work, not placed on a pedestal.

In practice, this means that knowledge requires a destination. Without a target, even the most brilliant insights scatter like light without a lens—bright, but unfocused and unable to ignite change. When knowledge is aligned with a concrete plan, it becomes directional. When it is paired with action, it becomes operational. And when it is reinforced by determination and commitment, it becomes transformational. Power emerges not from the possession of knowledge, but from the consistent, intentional application of that knowledge toward a specific, meaningful end.

This is why individuals with modest formal education often surpass highly credentialed graduates: they convert what they know—however limited—into purposeful action. They do not wait for ideal conditions, nor do they rely on the prestige of their qualifications. They act, they adapt, and they persist. Their knowledge, however humble, is always in motion. In contrast, many who hold advanced degrees fall into the illusion that knowledge alone entitles them to success. But knowledge without direction is like a ship without a compass—capable of movement, yet destined to drift. True power belongs to those who take what they know, define where they are going, and commit themselves fully to the journey.

How the Formula Becomes Transformational:

Power = Knowledge + Planning + Action × Determination and Commitment

When this formulation is applied intentionally, it becomes a blueprint for transformation in almost every aspect of one's life. Knowledge provides the raw material—the insight, the awareness, the understanding of what is possible. But knowledge alone does not move mountains. It must be paired with planning, which gives structure to intention and converts vague aspirations into clear, navigable pathways. Planning is where dreams acquire coordinates. It is where the abstract becomes actionable.

Action is the catalyst. Without action, even the most brilliant plan remains a silent document. Action breathes life into knowledge. It is the moment when ideas step out of the mind and enter the world. Yet action alone is not enough, because the world rarely rewards the first attempt. This is why determination and commitment multiply the entire equation. They are the force that sustains momentum when challenges arise, when progress slows, and when doubt whispers. Determination ensures continuity; commitment ensures completion.

When these elements operate together, they create transformation across personal, professional, and social domains. In one's career, this formula turns qualifications into influence and opportunities into achievements. In relationships, it transforms understanding into empathy, and empathy into meaningful connection. In health, it converts awareness into discipline, and discipline into vitality. In leadership, it turns vision into strategy, and strategy into impact. The formula is universal because it reflects a universal truth: power is not something one possesses—it is something one builds, step by step, through intentional application of what one knows.

Those who embrace this model stop waiting for circumstances to change and begin changing themselves. They stop relying on credentials and start relying on capability. They stop hoping for success and start engineering it. This is the essence of transformation: not a sudden leap, but a deliberate, sustained alignment of knowledge, planning, action, determination, and commitment. When these forces converge, they do not merely improve a life—they elevate it.

Action Plans and Daily Habits That Bring the Formula to Life:

1. Knowledge → Daily Learning with Purpose

Knowledge becomes transformative when it is curated, not consumed randomly.

<u>Daily Habits:</u>

- Spend 20–30 minutes each day learning something directly connected to your goals.
- Keep a "knowledge journal" where you record one insight per day and how you will apply it.
- Replace passive scrolling with intentional reading, listening, or observing.

<u>Action Plan:</u>

- Identify the 3–5 knowledge areas that matter most for your next stage of growth.
- Choose one primary learning source for each (books, courses, mentors, case studies).
- Review your progress weekly to ensure your learning aligns with your objectives.

2. Planning → Turning Intention into Structure

Planning is where clarity replaces chaos.

<u>Daily Habits:</u>

- Begin each morning by identifying your top three priorities.

- End each day with a 5-minute review: What moved you closer to your goal? What didn't?
- Use a simple weekly planning ritual every Sunday to map your next steps.

<u>Action Plan:</u>

- Break your long-term goal into quarterly, monthly, and weekly milestones.
- Create a "success map" that outlines what resources, skills, and actions you need.
- Schedule your priorities into your calendar—if it's not scheduled, it's not real.

3. Action → Consistent Movement Toward Your Target

Action is the bridge between knowing and becoming.

<u>Daily Habits:</u>

- Do one "needle-moving" task every day— something that directly advances your goal.
- Use the 10-minute rule: if a task feels overwhelming, commit to just 10 minutes.
- Track your actions, not just your intentions.

Action Plan:

- Identify the 20% of actions that will produce 80% of your results.
- Build a weekly accountability system—self-check, partner, or mentor.
- Remove friction: simplify your environment so action becomes the default.

4. Determination × Commitment → The Multipliers

These two forces amplify everything else. Without them, the formula collapses.

Daily Habits:

- Practice micro-discipline: small commitments kept daily build unshakeable resolve.
- Use affirmations or reminders that reinforce your purpose.
- Celebrate small wins to fuel momentum.

Action Plan:

- Define your "why" clearly and revisit it weekly.

- Create a resilience strategy: how you will respond when motivation dips.
- Set non-negotiables—behaviours you commit to regardless of mood or circumstance.

When These Forces Converge:

When knowledge, planning, action, determination, and commitment operate together, they create a compounding effect. You stop living reactively and start living architecturally. You become someone who:

- ✓ Learns with intention;
- ✓ Plans with clarity;
- ✓ Acts with consistency;
- ✓ Persists with resilience; and
- ✓ Commits with integrity.

And that is why, when these forces converge, they do not merely improve a life—they elevate it.

Final Thoughts:

For me, the author of this briefing, the formula *Power =
Knowledge + Planning + Action × Determination and
Commitment* is not merely an intellectual construct; it is the
very architecture of my life. I did not learn determination
from books, nor did commitment arrive as a gift. These
qualities were forged through fifty years of classical
Japanese martial arts—years of disciplined practice,
humility, and self-confrontation. When I recently marked
my 50th year of training at Nachi Falls in Wakayama, Japan,
I was reminded once again that true power is not something
one claims; it is something one cultivates through relentless
practice and purposeful living.

In the martial arts, knowledge is only the beginning. One
may memorize every kata (form), every principle, every
philosophical teaching, yet remain powerless if those
teachings are not embodied. The dojo teaches a simple
truth: *knowing is not doing.* Knowledge must be shaped by
planning—by the deliberate refinement of technique, the
intentional correction of one's weaknesses, and the

strategic cultivation of one's strengths. Every stance, every breath, every movement is a study in alignment. Without planning, knowledge remains scattered; with planning, it becomes direction.

But it is action that breathes life into all of this. A martial artist does not advance by thinking about training; they advance by stepping onto the tatami day after day, repeating a technique until it becomes part of their very being. And yet, even action is not enough. What has carried me through five decades of practice—through injuries, fatigue, doubt, and the long plateaus where progress seems invisible—has been determination and commitment. These are the multipliers in the formula. They are the forces that transform effort into mastery, and mastery into character.

This is why I say that martial arts did not simply teach me how to fight—they taught me how to live. They taught me that power is not found in knowledge alone, but in the disciplined, intentional application of that knowledge toward a defined purpose. When knowledge, planning, action, determination, and commitment converge, they do not merely improve a life—they elevate it. They elevate the practitioner. They elevate the human being. And ultimately, they elevate the world one disciplined act at a time. This understanding did not come to me from theory; it was carved into me through fifty years of classical Japanese martial arts—years of bowing, falling and again standing, years of repetition, years of confronting my own limitations beneath the mist of Nachi Falls.

In-Closing:

In the end, power is not what many imagine it to be. It is not position, prestige, or the illusion of control. True power is quieter, deeper, and far more demanding. It is the ability to direct one's knowledge with clarity, to shape one's actions with purpose, and to sustain one's path with unwavering determination and commitment. Power, in its truest form, is self-mastery. It is the discipline to act when comfort tempts you to stop, the courage to continue when progress is invisible, and the integrity to remain aligned with your purpose even when no one is watching. Knowledge gives direction, planning gives structure, action gives movement—but it is determination and commitment that give power its enduring shape. These forces, when united, do not simply strengthen a life; they elevate it. They elevate the individual beyond circumstance, beyond doubt, and beyond the limits they once believed were fixed.

This is the essence of power as I have come to understand it—not as something acquired, but as something cultivated. Not as an external force, but as an internal awakening. And when these forces converge, they do not merely improve a life—they transform it into a life of purpose, resilience, and quiet, unshakable strength.

For Further Insight and Practice:

HOW TO IMPROVE EMPATHY:
A NON-NEGOTIABLE LEADERSHIP SKILL

In Brief:

Empathy is now widely understood as an essential leadership capacity — not a soft add-on, but a core skill that strengthens communication, decision-making, and the overall health of teams. Leaders who practice empathy are better able to grasp how others see and experience situations, which in turn fosters clearer dialogue, deeper trust, and more effective collaboration. When people feel understood, they contribute more openly and work together with greater cohesion. Let us next examine this in more details.

The Two Dimensions:

Empathy itself has two distinct dimensions.

Cognitive Empathy: It involves the ability to comprehend another person's viewpoint — to intellectually step into their frame of reference.

Emotional Empathy: By contrast, is the capacity to sense and resonate with another's feelings. Both forms matter: one sharpens understanding, the other strengthens human connection.

Although some individuals may naturally lean toward empathy due to temperament or personality, it is not a fixed trait. Empathy can be cultivated and expanded through **neural plasticity** — the brain's ability to reorganize, adapt, and form new pathways. With intentional practice, reflection, and exposure to diverse perspectives, leaders can train themselves to become more attuned, more responsive, and ultimately more effective in how they relate to others.

Let us first discuss strengths and limitations of cognitive empathy, before we address emotional empathy and how to improve both of them.

Cognitive empathy, which is understanding someone's perspective, plays a crucial role in human interaction, particularly in communication, conflict resolution, and leadership. Unlike emotional empathy, which involves sharing another person's feelings, cognitive empathy focuses on recognizing and comprehending the thoughts, beliefs, and motivations that shape their experiences.

Strengths of Cognitive Empathy:

- **Facilitates Effective Communication:** By understanding another person's perspective, individuals can respond in ways that are more thoughtful and constructive, reducing misunderstandings.

- **Enhances Problem-Solving:** In professional and personal settings, cognitive empathy helps find solutions that consider multiple viewpoints, leading to more balanced decisions.

- **Supports Leadership and Negotiation:** Leaders and negotiators who apply cognitive empathy can better anticipate the needs and concerns of others, fostering collaboration and mutual respect.

Limitations and Potential Issues of Cognitive Empathy:

- **Can Be Emotionally Detached:** Unlike emotional empathy, cognitive empathy does not necessarily involve feeling what others feel. This detachment can sometimes lead to a lack of genuine compassion, making interactions feel calculated rather than heartfelt.

- **Potential for Manipulation:** In some cases, individuals with strong cognitive empathy but low emotional empathy can exploit their understanding of others for personal gain.

- **Challenges in Application:** Cognitive empathy requires intellectual effort and practice, particularly in complex or emotionally charged situations. Some individuals struggle to accurately interpret others' perspectives, leading to misjudgments.

Overall, cognitive empathy is a valuable skill that enhances interpersonal effectiveness, but *its limitations highlight the importance of balancing it with emotional and compassionate responses.* Now, with a view to the above, let us next take a look at emotional empathy.

As mentioned earlier, emotional empathy is the ability to feel someone else's emotions, this is a fundamental aspect of human connection. It enables people to experience and share the emotional states of others, fostering deep bonds and reinforcing social cohesion. Unlike cognitive empathy, which focuses on understanding perspectives, emotional empathy involves a visceral, instinctive response to another person's feelings.

Strengths of Emotional Empathy:

- **Strengthens Relationships:** Emotional empathy deepens personal connections by creating a sense of understanding and shared experience, making individuals feel seen and valued.

- **Encourages Compassionate Actions:** Feeling someone else's emotions often motivates people to help and support them, driving altruistic behavior.

- **Essential for Caregiving Professions:** Nurses, therapists, social workers, and other caregivers rely on emotional empathy to provide meaningful support, ensuring that their care is compassionate and responsive.

Limitations and Potential Issues of Emotional Empathy:

- **Can Be Overwhelming:** Some individuals experience "empathic distress", where they become emotionally consumed by others' suffering, leading to burnout or anxiety.

- **May Impair Objectivity:** Excessive emotional empathy can cloud judgment, making it difficult to assess situations rationally, especially in leadership or conflict resolution.

- **Selective Empathy:** People may feel empathy more strongly for individuals they relate to, potentially leading to biased perceptions and unequal treatment of others. Now that we are familiar with both components of empath, next, let us find out how we can improve our Neural Plasticity for better Cognitive and Emotional Empathy.

Improving neural plasticity can enhance cognitive and emotional empathy, allowing you to better understand and interpret others' perspectives and feelings. Here are some effective strategies:

1. Engage in Mindfulness and Meditation:

Practicing mindfulness and meditation can strengthen neural connections related to empathy and emotional regulation. Techniques like "Metta" meditation, aka, loving-kindness meditation have been shown to enhance compassion and perspective-taking.

2. Exercise Regularly:

Physical activities, especially 'aerobic' and 'anaerobic' (weightlifting) exercises stimulate the production of Brain-Derived Neurotrophic Factor (BDNF), which supports neural growth and adaptability. Activities like running, swimming, strength training, martial arts, and Yin yoga can improve cognitive flexibility and emotional awareness [1].

3. Challenge Your Brain with Learning:

Engaging in lifelong learning, such as: reading, learning a new language, practicing a new form of art, or solving puzzles, helps create new neural pathways. Exposure to diverse perspectives through literature or discussions can also strengthen cognitive empathy.

4. Prioritize Quality Sleep:

Sleep plays a crucial role in consolidating new neural connections. Deep sleep enhances memory and emotional processing, *making it easier to understand others' viewpoints.*

5. Maintain a Brain-Healthy Diet:

Consuming foods rich in omega-3 fatty acids, antioxidants, and vitamins supports brain function. Curcumin, found in turmeric, has been linked to improved neuroplasticity and brain regulatory function [2].

6. Foster Social Connections:

Interacting with diverse groups and practicing active listening can strengthen neural pathways related to empathy. Engaging in *meaningful conversations and volunteering* can enhance your ability to understand different perspectives.

Conclusion:

Cognitive and emotional empathy are both essential because they shape how we connect, communicate, and support others. This is crucial in professional settings, negotiations, and problem-solving, where understanding someone's thoughts can lead to better collaboration and decision-making. Ignoring either component of empathy can lead to misunderstandings, strained relationships, and a lack of emotional intelligence. A balance between both ensures that we not only understand others, but also genuinely care about their experiences.

References:

1. Empathetic Brain Rewiring, (nd), Mindlab Neuroscience, https://mindlabneuroscience.com/empathetic-brain-rewiring/

2. The Role of Neuroplasticity in Developing Emotional Intelligence, (2024), Neuoba, https://www.neuroba.com/post/the-role-of-neuroplasticity-in-developing-emotional-intelligence-neuroba

For Further Insight and Practice:

LIVING ABROAD: FINDING YOUR PURPOSE

In Brief:

As an executive consultant who visited, worked in, and experienced 22 countries, I have gained invaluable insights into diverse business landscapes, cultural dynamics, geo-political and global market trends, which shaped my perspective on adaptability, resilience, and personal growth. In my professional journey, I have learned that true success in a foreign environment comes from a willingness to integrate, an openness to change, and a deep respect for the traditions and values of the local community. However, for those who wish to be a permanent immigrant and call their new environment 'home', the success requires a deeper level of self-awareness and understanding of their new environment.

Living abroad is a unique opportunity to redefine yourself, reinvent your identity, and build a life that truly aligns with your aspirations. To achieve this, you must first define your purpose—and no, you can't simply think it through in your head. *You need to put your thoughts on paper and engage in deep, reflective writing.*

Many people say to me, "I've thought about it, but I just can't find my purpose!" or "What if I never discover my purpose?" My immediate response? You're not searching deep enough. What you're looking for isn't on the surface— so dig deeper, focus intently, and even meditate on it.

Some, eager for a quick answer, ask, "What is my purpose here on Earth?" I always reply, **"Your purpose is to find your purpose!"** While others may offer guidance, only you can truly discover it.

How to Begin:

Take the time to understand your values—culturally, financially, and within the context of your new environment, i.e. your host country. What truly matters to you? What matters to your new community? Are your values aligned with this environment, or do they clash? Can you identify shared values? Can you offer something valuable that your new community will appreciate?

Additionally, consider what sets you apart. What unique skills, perspectives, or experiences do you have that others in your new environment may lack? As you reflect and jot down your thoughts, remain open-minded and embrace change. Be honest in recognizing your shortcomings, as these may hinder your ability to survive or eventually thrive.

Remember what you learned in biology: **"A living organism is shaped by its environment."** *You, too, are a living creature shaped by your surroundings and environment.* Now that you're in a different environment, you must accept the process of adaptation—the challenges, hardships, and emotional toll it may bring. Despite all, you must embrace the journey with **'military grade discipline'**. *If you refuse to adapt to your new surroundings or reject the culture, survival in this new environment will be extremely difficult—it's a simple fact of biology.*

Steps to Take:

Most people immigrate for better opportunities, an improved standard of living, and a brighter future. But you must remember: to achieve these goals, embracing change is crucial. Keep this in mind: ***If you do what you did, you'll get what you got.*** If you continue doing what you've always done unsuccessfully, you'll keep getting the same results.

As a living being naturally shaped by your environment, you shouldn't expect to maintain the same mindset, attitude, behaviors, and lifestyle from your native country while hoping that success, comfort, and prosperity will come effortlessly.

1. Reflect deeply to identify your purpose in life.

2. Set specific goals that will help fulfill your purpose.

3. Determine what you need to learn, adjust, and adopt to equip yourself for success—then start learning, adjusting, and adopting as quickly as possible.

4. Assign time-bound deadlines for each goal, along with periodic evaluations to assess progress.

5. Celebrate each milestone and take pride in your achievements—acknowledge your growth and recognize how far you've come.

Since fulfilling your purpose leads to fulfillment in life—and ultimately the happiness you seek—everything you do should align with that purpose. *Keep your focus sharp and remain committed to your purpose.*

Staying aligned with your purpose also means learning to navigate distractions with discipline and grace. Life will inevitably present competing demands, shifting priorities, and moments of uncertainty, but a clear sense of purpose acts as an internal compass that keeps you oriented toward what truly matters. When your daily choices reflect your deeper intentions, you cultivate a life that feels coherent, meaningful, and self-directed. Over time, this alignment becomes not just a practice, but a way of being—one that sustains your growth and strengthens your sense of fulfillment.

For Further Insight and Practice:

WOMEN'S RIGHTS: A UNIVERSAL MANDATE

In Brief:

All human beings are born free and equal in dignity and rights. Among these rights is the fundamental freedom to live without violence, discrimination, or coercion. Yet gender inequality continues to shape social, political, and economic realities in ways that disproportionately harm women and girls. Despite decades of advocacy and progress, women around the world still face gender-based violence, sexual harassment, arbitrary detention, and targeted persecution simply because of their gender.

No country has fully achieved gender justice, and in many regions—particularly parts of the Middle East, the birthplace of the major monotheistic traditions—women's liberty remains severely constrained. Deeply entrenched patriarchal norms, reinforced by rigid interpretations of religious doctrine, are often used to justify the systematic denial of women's rights. Under extremist ideologies and authoritarian regimes, discriminatory laws govern nearly every stage of a woman's life: from birth and childhood to appearance, education, work, marriage, parenting, divorce, custody, and even the rituals surrounding death.

In such environments, women's autonomy is not merely restricted; it is actively suppressed. Yet it is precisely within these oppressive conditions that the courage of women who resist becomes even more remarkable. Their determination to claim their rights—often at great personal risk—stands as a powerful testament to human resilience and the universal desire for freedom.

Understanding these realities underscores the importance of knowing and asserting the rights enshrined in the Universal Declaration of Human Rights. It is a reminder that equality is not a privilege granted by society, but a birthright that must be protected, upheld, and continually defended.

How to Ensure Women's Rights:

Ensuring that women's rights are respected requires action at multiple levels — legal, institutional, cultural, and personal. No single measure is sufficient on its own; meaningful protection emerges when these layers reinforce one another and create an environment where equality is both expected and enforced.

1. Strong Legal Protections and Enforcement:

Countries must adopt laws that explicitly prohibit discrimination, violence, and unequal treatment. Just as important is enforcement: police, courts, and public institutions must apply these laws consistently and without bias. Legal reforms lose their power if they are not implemented with integrity.

2. Education and Public Awareness:

Societies that understand women's rights as human rights are more likely to uphold them. Education — from school curricula to public campaigns — helps dismantle harmful stereotypes, challenge patriarchal norms, and promote gender equality as a shared social value rather than a niche concern.

3. Empowering Women Economically and Politically:

When women have access to education, employment, financial independence, and leadership roles, their rights become harder to ignore or suppress. Representation in decision-making bodies ensures that policies reflect women's lived realities and priorities.

4. Holding Governments and Institutions Accountable:

International bodies, civil-society organizations, and human-rights monitors play a crucial role in tracking violations and pressuring governments to uphold global standards. Transparency, reporting mechanisms, and independent oversight help prevent abuses from being hidden or normalized.

5. Supporting Grassroots Movements and Women's Voices:

Local activists, community leaders, and women's rights organizations often drive the most meaningful change. Their work must be protected, funded, and amplified. When women can speak freely and organize safely, societies become more resilient and more just.

6. Engaging Men and Boys as Allies:

Gender equality cannot be achieved by women alone. Men and boys must be part of the cultural shift — challenging harmful norms, rejecting violence, and advocating for fairness in their families, workplaces, and communities.

7. Creating Safe Reporting and Support Systems:

Survivors of violence and discrimination need accessible, confidential, and trustworthy avenues to seek help. Shelters, hotlines, legal aid, and trauma-informed services ensure that women are not left alone when their rights are violated.

Respecting women's rights is not a single action but a sustained commitment to justice, dignity, and equality. When societies invest in these protections, they strengthen not only the lives of women and girls but the moral and democratic fabric of the entire community.

What Individuals Can Do to Safeguard Women's Rights:

Safeguarding women's rights at the individual level is both powerful and necessary. Structural change matters, but it is often the everyday choices of ordinary people that create the cultural conditions in which rights are either upheld or violated. When individuals act with awareness, courage, and consistency, they help build communities where equality is not merely an aspiration but a lived reality.

1. Educate Yourself and Others:

Understanding women's rights, gender equality, and the realities women face is the first step. Read widely, listen to women's experiences, and challenge misinformation when you encounter it. Knowledge equips you to speak up with confidence and clarity.

2. Challenge Discrimination and Harmful Norms:

Sexist jokes, stereotypes, and dismissive attitudes may seem small, but they reinforce larger systems of inequality. Interrupt them when you can. Model respectful behavior and encourage others to do the same. Cultural change begins with everyday interactions.

3. Support Women's Voices and Leadership:

Amplify women's contributions in workplaces, communities, and public spaces. Advocate for their inclusion in decision-making roles. When women's voices are heard, policies and practices become more equitable.

4. Believe and Support Survivors of Violence

If someone discloses harassment or abuse, respond with empathy and without judgment. Encourage them to seek professional help if they choose to, and respect their autonomy. Social support is a critical factor in healing and safety.

5. Promote Equal Opportunities:

In your workplace, school, or community, advocate for fair hiring, equal pay, parental leave, and safe working environments. Small acts—such as mentoring women or calling out bias in meetings—can shift institutional culture.

6. Engage Men and Boys as Allies:

Encourage conversations about respect, consent, and equality. Men who model healthy, equitable behavior help dismantle harmful norms and create safer environments for everyone.

7. Support Women's Rights Organizations:

Donate, volunteer, or amplify their work. Grassroots groups often operate with limited resources but have immense impact on legal reform, survivor support, and community education.

8. Vote and Advocate for Gender-Just Policies:

Use your civic voice to support leaders and policies that protect women's rights. Public pressure influences governments, institutions, and corporations to uphold equality.

9. Practice Everyday Respect and Equality:

Treat women as full and equal human beings in all contexts—professional, social, and personal. Respect boundaries, share responsibilities, and value their autonomy.

How Firms and Corporations Can Safeguard Women's Rights:

Firms and corporations play a decisive role in shaping whether women's rights are upheld in everyday life. Because workplaces are microcosms of society — and often the primary sites of economic participation, leadership development, and social interaction — corporate behavior can either reinforce inequality or actively dismantle it. When companies commit to gender equity, they not only protect women's rights but also strengthen their own performance, culture, and long-term sustainability.

1. Establish Clear Anti-Discrimination and Anti-Harassment Policies:

Companies must adopt explicit, zero-tolerance policies against gender-based discrimination, harassment, and violence. These policies should be communicated clearly, enforced consistently, and supported by confidential reporting mechanisms that protect employees from retaliation.

2. Ensure Equal Pay and Fair Promotion Practices:

Closing gender pay gaps and ensuring transparent promotion criteria are essential. Regular pay audits, standardized evaluation processes, and accountability for managers help prevent bias and ensure that women advance based on merit, not stereotypes or informal networks.

3. Create Safe, Inclusive, and Respectful Work Environments:

Workplaces should be designed to support dignity and safety — from equitable parental leave and flexible work arrangements to safe facilities and respectful communication norms. Training on unconscious bias, consent, and inclusive leadership helps build a culture where women feel valued and protected.

4. Invest in Women's Leadership and Professional Development:

Mentorship programs, leadership pipelines, and targeted training opportunities help women access senior roles where they remain underrepresented. When women lead, corporate decisions become more balanced, ethical, and reflective of diverse perspectives.

5. Support Work–Life Balance and Care Responsibilities:

Women often carry disproportionate caregiving burdens. Corporations can mitigate this by offering flexible schedules, remote-work options, childcare support, and equitable parental leave for all genders. These policies reduce burnout and enable women to thrive professionally.

6. Hold Leadership Accountable for Gender Equality:

Executives and managers must be evaluated not only on financial performance but also on their commitment to diversity, equity, and inclusion. When gender equality becomes a leadership act, it becomes a priority rather than a slogan.

7. Partner with Women's Rights and Community Organizations:

Corporations can amplify their impact by collaborating with NGOs, advocacy groups, and community initiatives that support women's rights. These partnerships strengthen social responsibility and extend corporate influence beyond the workplace.

8. Promote Ethical Supply Chains:

Companies must ensure that their suppliers uphold labor rights, prohibit exploitation, and protect women from unsafe conditions. Ethical sourcing audits and transparent reporting help prevent abuses such as forced labor, harassment, or discriminatory practices in global supply chains.

Conclusion:

Safeguarding women's rights requires a shared commitment across every layer of society. Individuals shape the cultural norms that either uphold dignity or permit discrimination; institutions and governments create the legal and structural frameworks that protect freedoms; and corporations influence the economic and social environments in which women live and work.

When these forces operate in alignment, they form a powerful ecosystem of accountability and respect. Gender equality is not achieved through isolated efforts but through the collective will to challenge injustice, dismantle harmful norms, and build systems that honor the full humanity of women and girls. Protecting women's rights is therefore not only a legal or moral obligation — it is a measure of our shared progress and a reflection of the world we choose to create together.

The Author's Final Note:

A BRIDGE OF LIGHT

Thoughts Carried by a Poem

A Bridge of Light:

In lands where voices clash and cry,
Where difference draws a wary eye,
Let hearts be lanterns in the night—
To guide the way with gentle light.

Not every path is paved the same,
Not every soul speaks one name.
But in the hush between the words,
A deeper truth is often heard.

Understanding is a patient seed,
It grows not fast, but meets a need.
It asks not for a perfect face,
But listens closely and grants its grace.

Tolerance is the quiet art...
Of holding space for every heart.
It does not bend to hate or fear,
But stands with love, sincere and clear.

So let us build, not walls, but wings,
And learn the song that kindness sings.
For when we choose to truly see,
We shape a world where all are free.

Mosi Dorbayani

About the Author:

Dr. Mosi Dorbayani is an integrative executive-scholar bridging consultancy, jurisprudence, counselling, and cultural neuroscience—advancing reflective praxis across law, diplomacy, governance, economics, cognitive science, and pedagogy.

With advanced degrees from Harvard, Aston, Sunderland, Wolverhampton, and Salford universities, he has consulted for multinational firms including KPMG, BNP Paribas, and Sony-Ericsson, offering training, coaching, and insight into organizational and leadership development, governance, and strategic foresight. He is author of 22 books, an award-winning scholar, and a multi-platinum award-winning songwriter.

For his full profile visit:
https://www.dorbayani.com/mosidorbayaniprofile

LinkedIn: linkedin.com/in/mosidorbayani

Also From This Author:

Cultural Neuroscience
An Investigative Study of Cultural Activities and Their Impact on
Brain and Emotional Behavior

MOSI DORBAYANI, PhD
Member of:
Canadian Psychological Association

LAW AND CULTURAL DIPLOMACY:

The Cohabitation of International Law, and International Cultural Interactions

MOSI DORBAYANI, PhD
Member of International Bar Association - IBA

BUSINESS
SAMURAI
SKILLS AND STRATEGIES FOR
LEADERS &
ENTREPRENEURS

リーダーシップ

Available at
amazon

BARNES
&NOBLE

MOSI DORBAYANI

TALENT-BASED ECONOMY

Talent Development & Leadership Succession Strategies:
A Sustainable Business Economics Act

MOSI DORBAYANI

Mosi Dorbayani

MESSAGE SONG

DELIVERING IMPORTANT AND POWERFUL MESSAGES
THROUGH LYRICS AND MUSIC

Kindle Edition List:

The Kindle edition of each briefing is available from Amazon – Kindle eBook worldwide:

THE MOST HANGING QUESTION IN PUBLIC FINANCE AND POLITICAL ECONOMY

ASIN: B0GKBS1YHC

THE COADUNATE ECONOMIC MODEL: A REFLECTION IN MY OWN VOICE

ASIN: B0GKJ9Q4M3

THE GRAMMAR OF BELONGING: THE NEUROPSYCHOLOGICAL FOUNDATIONS OF TOGETHERNESS

ASIN: B0GKQFR4KR

THE NEUROPSYCHOLOGY OF CIVIC HEALTH

ASIN: B0GLKXNT4F

THE PSYCHOLOGICAL IMPACT OF AUTOMATION ON TEAMS: NEUROSCIENCE AT THE CROSSROADS OF PROGRESS AND PURPOSE

ASIN: B0GMT9L5GK

WHERE LAW LIVES IN CULTURE

ASIN: B0FQJMX9RR

UNESCO CONVENTIONS AND STATE BEHAVIOR

ASIN: B0GM2L374W

INTERNATIONAL LAW AND THE SOVEREIGNTY OF SMALL
AND VULNERABLE STATES

ASIN: B0GN5K1XQD

DIPLOMACY WITHOUT A PULSE: A MANIFESTO FOR RE-
HUMANIZING STATECRAFT

ASIN: B0GL9JGSXH

CULTURAL DIPLOMACY IN THE AGE OF AI: AI'S IMPACT ON
CULTURAL IDENTITY AND PUBLIC DIALOGUE

ASIN: B0GN5FPP95

ADAPTIVE CROSS-CULTURAL NEGOTIATION: THE
DIAGNOSTIC FOUNDATIONS IN DIPLOMACY

ASIN: B0GN54ZYRW

POLICY IN A SHARED WORLD: ALIGNING NATIONS,
ADVANCING HUMANITY

ASIN: B0GKFM1XM5

The Author Central:

https://www.amazon.com/stores/Mosi-Dorbayani/author/B06XHSGN6M

The List of References for Briefing 6:

Bercovitch, J., & Jackson, R. (2009). Conflict resolution in the twenty-first century: Principles, methods, and approaches. University of Michigan Press.

Farrell, H., & Newman, A. L. (2019). Weaponized interdependence: How global economic networks shape state coercion. International Security, 44(1), 42–79.

Katzenstein, P. J. (1996). The culture of national security: Norms and identity in world politics. Columbia University Press.

Permanent Court of Arbitration. (2016). The South China Sea arbitration (The Republic of the Philippines v. The People's Republic of China), PCA Case No. 2013-19: Award of 12 July 2016. https://pca-cpa.org

Slaughter, A.-M. (2004). A new world order. Princeton University Press.

United Nations Conference on Trade and Development. (2021). Digital economy report 2021: Cross-border data flows and development – For whom the data flow. United Nations. https://unctad.org